PRAISE FOR

FrameShifting

From the Foreword: "What Alison and Mary have done is to illuminate the discipline of problem framing and using frameworks effectively, making what has historically been more of an art into a learnable science that consultants of all flavors can use to increase the impact of their work with clients.

However, this book is not just for consultants. It's for any businessperson who wants to learn to solve gnarly problems—and, importantly, to solve the right problems—with greater insight and rigor. And, importantly, it's for collaborators who want to engage others in the exploration and solving of tough problems. *FrameShifting* is as much a collaboration approach as it is a problem-solving approach."

—Melissa Quinn, Innovation Advisor and Coach, former COO and Managing Director, Doblin, a Deloitte business

"In today's dynamic world, we are constantly faced with new, complicated, transverse problems to solve. *FrameShifting* provides pragmatic insights not only on how to frame the problem for success, but also how to leverage the right framework and the power of a collaborative team to create winning solutions."

—Scott Clark, Executive Vice President & Member of the Group Executive Committee at Michelin

"As the CEO or strategic leader this gem of a book will leave you feeling confident and well equipped in utilizing frameworks (often without the cost of an external consultant) to solve those nagging complex and systemic problems that keep you up at night! I will be sharing this with all my CEO colleagues."

—Marne Keller-Krikava, Founder & President at Invest In Her Foundation, former President & CEO J. J. Keller & Associates, Inc.

"As a product of the Harvard Business School and the Boston Consulting Group, using frameworks for problem solving and communicating with my teams has become part of my DNA. Reading *FrameShifting* had a profound impact, and made me realize that I have been looking at frameworks in only two dimensions. I have been missing the third dimension that comes from the collective perspectives provided by my team members who can help me shape and enrich the framework. The archetypes Alison and Mary portray accurately represent the behaviors we all find on our teams. Harnessed the right way, their perspectives will greatly improve the fit of any framework and its ultimate success in delivering the desired results."

—David S. Boone, CEO at United Allergy Services, Director at Sawtooth Growth Partners and National Western Life

"WHAT A GREAT BOOK!!! I quickly realized I needed a highlighter and pen to make notes in the margins. I could see consultants we should not have worked with, and also see why we sometimes get stuck within our teams. When I can apply and relate immediately to a book, that gets my juices and mind going. Post *FrameShifting*, I find myself approaching situations with a heightened desire to understand, plan and choose the best next step . . . not necessarily the step I am most comfortable with. This is a shift for me. I think I will be revisiting *FrameShifting* physically and mentally for years to come."

—Michelle Devine Giese, CEO at Apricity – a progressive recovery community

"*FrameShifting* offers a powerful concept that enables individuals at all levels of an organization, to more effectively develop decision-making prowess within the context of an external world racing toward an ever increasing pace of evolution. *FrameShifting* offers an intuitive, easy to understand process for escaping the confinement of existing decision-making frameworks and moving toward the intelligent use of approaches that better fit today's world. I was able to put it to use immediately."

—Jeffrey Resnick, Chief Operating Officer at NAXION

"*FrameShifting* goes well beyond sharing the importance of frameworks in solving today's business challenges. Whether existing or newly conceived, *FrameShifting* offers practical methods for validating a framework's fitness for your particular situation and building a collaborative team that leverages each individual's unique skills. The result? More innovative, shared solutions."

—Jim Heininger, Founder and Principal at Dixon|James Communications

"Leave it to Alison and Mary to create the book we need right now. *FrameShifting*—a strategic and practical approach on collaboration and problem solving is a must read. It creates the right amount of structure and perspective to not only identify how to solve a problem, but also how to engage all types of thinkers in your company to help solve it. So often our teammates have the answers we need as leaders if we are brave enough to listen, collaborate and create shared stories of our future together."

—Kirsten Benefiel, HSS Chief Executive Officer, Founding Member of the Colorado Inclusive Economy

"*FrameShifting* is also its own framework for figuring out how to make sure the right people are working in the right ways to solve the right problems. *FrameShifting* is to collaboration what sanding, patching and priming are to painting a room: the necessary foundation for getting the job done right."

—Brad Brinegar, Chairman at McKinney, Executive in Residence at Duke University

FrameShifting

FrameShifting

Unleashing the power of frameworks to
fuel collaboration and solve tough problems

ALISON HEISER & MARY O'CONNOR SHAW

Printed in the United States of America
First Printing, 2020

Route 10 Press

Library of Congress Cataloging-in-Publication Data is Available:
ISBN 978-0-578-78111-2 (paperback)
ISBN 978-0-578-78112-9 (ebook)

To all the problems that have kept me up at night,
and to Jim for understanding.
—*Alison*

To my mother, Kathleen, for everything,
and to Sidney for everything else.
—*Mary*

Contents

Foreword

only met Alison five years ago, but she's got that kind of warmth that makes you feel like you've known her forever. One of my earliest memories is of us sipping coffee at an outdoor café at the corner of East Wacker Drive and Michigan Avenue in Chicago. I'd just made the decision to leave my job as COO of Doblin, Deloitte's design and innovation practice, and start my own coaching and training practice to help leaders develop their innovation skills. Alison was someone who'd run her own successful business coaching and collaborating with senior executives for many years, and I was hoping to pick her brain on how to get started. She generously shared her experience with me.

When the conversation turned to what was next for her, she mused about how she could take her practice to the next level . . . to help even more leaders in more organizations tackle "wicked problems."

"You should write a book," I said.

"A book?" Alison seemed unconvinced. "I don't think I could write a book."

I probed on this a little, skeptical that a woman who has held incredible leadership roles in prominent companies and built her own thriving consulting practice wouldn't have very interesting insights and stories for a book. I asked Alison to describe how she helped her clients, and she proceeded to tell me about the ways that she brought a combination of structure and creativity to help clients see problems in new and different ways in order to help them get "unstuck" and achieve great results. While Alison modestly saw this as just "how she worked," it sure sounded like a methodology about problem-solving that would be valuable for any leader to learn. And it definitely sounded like a book I'd want to read.

It turns out, Alison does have great insights and stories for a book . . . and the proof is in the pages you're about to explore! After taking some time to figure out how to pull the methodologies and approaches that come quite naturally to her out of her own head, Alison partnered with Mary O'Connor Shaw, an amazing graphic artist and storyteller, and soon thereafter, *FrameShifting*™ was born. *FrameShifting* is a unique user-centered guide to framing problems effectively and using frameworks to generate the right insights to solve them.

Now I've been working in professional services for my entire twenty-five-year career, so I'm no stranger to frameworks. In fact, I spent my first fifteen years at Monitor Group, co-founded by the esteemed Michael Porter, whose Five Forces analytic tool is perhaps *the* most famous business framework of all time. Frameworks are the underpinnings of the entire consulting industry. And almost everyone has an opinion on them. Some people want them to be front and center. In fact, in consulting firm interviews, candidates who do not actively structure their thinking into some sort of logical framework get dinged for it. At the same time, too many frameworks can be overwhelming, leading to "framework overload." Their overuse has, at times, made frameworks the butt of consulting-industry jokes. I had one colleague who felt that while frameworks were valuable behind the scenes, they should never be obvious in the final deliverable, and he was known for deriding colleagues with the phrase "How embarrassing . . . Your framework is showing!"

What's clear is that frameworks *can* be very useful, yet no one really talks about how to use them effectively as a tool for problem solving. Sure, you can be trained on how to deploy a specific framework, but how you learn to do the difficult work of problem framing and of choosing or creating the right framework for the task at hand is something of a mystery in the business world. Many great consultants learn to do this by working closely with someone like Alison, who does it very intuitively. They pick it up through some sort of osmotic process.

What Alison and Mary have done is illuminate the discipline of problem framing and using frameworks effectively, making what has historically been more of an art into a learnable science that consultants of all flavors can use to increase the impact of their work with clients.

However, this book is not just for consultants. It's for any businessperson who wants to learn to solve gnarly problems—and, importantly, to solve the *right* problems—with greater insight and rigor. And, importantly, it's for collaborators who want to engage others in the exploration and solving of tough problems. FrameShifting is as much a collaboration approach as it is a problem-solving approach.

And a big part of what makes us great as collaborators is understanding more about ourselves. FrameShifting helps with that, too. In fact, Alison and Mary have created four archetypes that help each of us identify our own problem-solving propensities so that we can be aware of the ways in which we can enable, and unintentionally hinder, our own collaboration and problem-solving efforts.

Once in a while we are lucky enough to peek inside the brains of smart, wonderful thinkers, and in doing so, we are able to up our own games. I'm so thrilled that, through *FrameShifting*, Alison and Mary have afforded us such an opportunity.

I wish you all exciting challenges and successful FrameShifting!

Melissa Quinn, Innovation Advisor and Coach,
former COO and Managing Director, Doblin, a Deloitte business

Introduction: The Origins of FrameShifting

*A*fter she spent the first half of her working life as a marketing leader, Alison Heiser pivoted to consulting as a second act. As a senior executive she focused on getting results; as a consultant she continues to think like a client.

Soon after joining Accenture, the global technology consulting firm, Alison was invited to coffee with two senior partners. She was preparing for a meeting with the CEO of one of Accenture's most important clients, and the partners wanted to know her framework for addressing his company's situation. She didn't think she had a framework, she said; she just understood his challenge and how to help him. But the partners told Alison that simply wasn't good enough. They coached her to dig a little deeper and translate her implicit thinking into an explicitly defined method. In a nutshell, success at a consulting firm depends on developing skills as a FrameBuilder.

Advice heeded, Alison created the "Branded Customer Experience" framework, which was shared with the client's CEO and set in motion a series of projects in each of the framework areas to activate the strategy. When the CEO embraced the framework, the senior partners were validated, and the collaboration raised everyone's game. It was a big win, and it felt good.

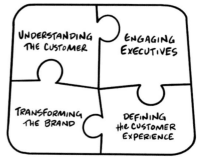

Fast-forward to today, and Alison still gets the same question: What is her framework for clients? Only now she has a different answer. It's not that she doesn't have a framework . . . *it's just not necessarily "hers."* Over time she's become adept at discovering and leveraging any number of frameworks, depending on the situation. And this "depending on the situation" is really all about provocative framing. Alison's client mindset gives her a pragmatic, results orientation— and the belief that when her work with clients is successful, then her consulting business will also be successful.

It turns out that this agnostic approach—applying frameworks intelligently—is an incredibly useful leadership skill, and also remarkably rare. In a chance meeting with Philip Kotler from Northwestern University's Kellogg School of Management, Alison shared her story with him:

I started my career at P&G, where they had a process and a method for everything . . . along with people to make sure you understood the P&G way and followed the discipline. After leaving P&G, my calling card was the P&G experience . . . yet I quickly understood that my new employers did not want to roll over to P&G approaches. They had their own ways of doing business, and from my earliest days in transition I was acutely aware of the need to simultaneously adapt to a new company, while finding ways to bring in new perspectives. I never became wedded to a particular process, template, or method . . . I became focused on getting results.

After hearing her story, Kotler told Alison, "You should write a book."

Soon after that, Alison met Melissa Quinn and described her journey as a consultant and the nagging feeling that she was not following the typical consulting path of designing and championing her own framework. Like Kotler, Melissa pointed out the uniqueness of Alison's approach and encouraged her to embrace it in her work advising senior leaders.

And that's when Melissa told Alison, "You should write a book."

When Mary O'Connor Shaw heard these stories, she not only echoed their encouragement, but unexpectedly and fortuitously volunteered to be Alison's writing partner and visual storyteller. After a day on Mary's farm discussing their goals and aspirations for the project, Alison and Mary toasted to their new partnership, and the book took flight.

Together, Mary and Alison have codified this leadership skill into a language and methodology they call FrameShifting. FrameShifting is a skill that can be learned, and with practice it will step change how leaders and teams collaborate to solve the thorny challenges in any organization.

Who this book is for

In the pages of this book are stories of people like you—the go-to people who are the lifeblood of an organization, recruited to join project teams, challenged to solve wicked problems and to envision the future. You know who you are. You might be a senior executive, a team leader, a subject matter expert, a deep thinker, a newly minted graduate. Perhaps you call yourself innovative, perhaps you don't. All the same, you are changing the status quo and propelling organizations forward.

And if you're like most of the leaders we work with, your world and the challenges you face don't look anything like the stuff of college textbooks. It seems like every new startup is born to disrupt something. New technologies are transforming anything and everything. A global pandemic changes how we work, shop, eat, and gather. Nothing is safe. Nothing feels stable. Which explains why yesterday's problem-solving methods aren't working like they used to. Yet far too often we see teams of hard-working people using those familiar, tried-and-true tools and frameworks, only to become frustrated when progress eludes them. Old habits die hard.

It's no wonder there's such a hunger to learn new skills and a nearly universal desire to "think differently." But how? Simply knowing that you need to be more flexible and adaptable doesn't tell you anything about how to do it. And then there's the need to collaborate. While collaboration is practically a given expectation, it involves a lot more than simply sequestering a bunch of smart people in a room and telling them to be innovative.

Unfortunately, the "smart-people-in-a-room" approach is more common than you might think. But a team without a framework quickly swirls and loses momentum. This explains, at least in part, the mixed feelings about collaboration. While most agree it's a good thing, if not properly structured, collaboration can absorb a lot of time with little to show for the effort.

"Time is really the only capital that any human being has, and the thing that he can least afford to waste or lose." *—Thomas Edison*

So, what is a leader to do? A logical response to this dilemma is to hire a consultant. If you have chosen this route, you are not alone, and you know that a consultant's advice is not cheap. The global consulting sector is one of the service industry's largest and most mature markets. Yet a consultant can bring tremendous value—providing specific expertise and dedicated resources with focus, discipline, and a sense of urgency around key milestones.

A more common approach is the DIY alternative—reading relevant books, articles, and whitepapers. Whether your browsing arena of choice is Google, Amazon, or the business section of your local bookstore, a quick search will turn up hundreds—thousands, actually—of titles written by academics and consultants, each with a preferred framework and a promise to help you "get there" quickly and efficiently.

Over time, the most influential consultants become synonymous with the frameworks they develop. You can probably name a favorite right off the top of your head: Philip Kotler's 4Ps in marketing or perhaps Michael Porter's Five Forces in competitive strategy. In books like these, the framework is the hero, and the author is both the situation expert and the solution creator. Companies also create frameworks: The Boston Consulting Group famously developed the product portfolio matrix with stars, cash cows, question marks, and dogs. Let's be clear—these thought leaders are successful for a reason: their thinking is sound, and their frameworks work . . . if you know *how* and *when* to apply them, that is. And there's the rub.

FrameShifting describes a new leadership skill set that is like four-wheel drive for teams stuck in the swirl of debate, a limiting mindset, or a one-size-fits-all solution that just doesn't fit. It is borne of empathy from listening to hundreds of clients express these very typical concerns:

> *"I thought I was clear with the project goals, but the team just doesn't get it."*

> *"You'd think with all these smart people in the room, we could just figure it out."*

> *"We seem to think that our favorite methodology can solve anything."*

> *"Oh, no—here comes my boss with another book she's just read."*

> *"We keep having the same debates, and we're swirling."*

> *"It seems like our management listens to consultants when we've already thought of it."*

If any of these statements resonates, this book is for you. In clear, concise language, we detail practical methods for framing a problem, choosing a framework relevant to the situation, and using optimal ways to use and share a framework effectively. Our practitioner's approach is unique in that it is simultaneously human-centered—*designed for people on teams*—and framework-agnostic—*not wedded to a particular framework.*

FrameShifting is a "framework for frameworks"—a user's guide to understanding and applying these powerful tools. Whether you are tasked with solving your organization's latest challenge or with finding and exploiting new business growth opportunities, learning to FrameShift will help you transform counterproductive team behaviors into an adaptive mindset that will enable you to achieve the high-impact results that are often so elusive.

FrameShifting is based on a belief that there is a more useful and intelligent path to leveraging the frameworks of leading consultants—a companion guide to all those books you've been reading. Our approach is fundamentally about building skills with teams and working with them to own the frame, the framework, and the solution. Our goal is to prepare the team to "fly on their own." This is without a doubt an ideal way to get results.

Whether you are a team leader, team sponsor, or team player, changing the way you collaborate will also lift your energy level and engender optimism. Laughter is an important signal that things are moving in the right direction. We hope you have fun learning to FrameShift!

Part 1

FrameShifting Overview

FrameShifting Map

Start HERE

> I KNOW THERE'S AN OPPORTUNITY IN THERE...

OPPORTUNITY LANDSCAPE

TAKE THE QUIZ

MEET the ARCHETYPES

FRAME THE PROBLEM

OOPS! DIDN'T QUITE NAIL IT... REFRAME

FRAMING METHODS
- 360° ALIGNMENT
- EXTERNAL FLIP
- DISCOVERY SESSION

FRAME CHECK

CHECKLIST

SIGNS OF A POWERFUL FRAME
✓ EVERYONE CAN NAME THE FRAME
✓ PROJECT NAME ≠ OPPORTUNITY FRAME
✓ STORYTELLING IS RICH & WIDESPREAD
✓ TEAM EMBRACES EVOLVING FRAME

FRAMEWORK CHECK

SIGNS OF A POWERFUL FRAMEWORK

✓ TEAM CAN DESCRIBE THE FRAMEWORK
✓ WORK SESSIONS ARE FOCUSED & PRODUCTIVE
✓ MEETINGS END ON TIME & DEADLINES ARE MET
✓ SOLUTIONS ARE INNOVATIVE, RELEVANT & INSPIRING!

FRAMEWORK TOOLKIT

YIKES!

FRAMEWORK DOESN'T FIT... TRY AGAIN!

SELECT THE FRAMEWORK

STORYTELLING with IMPACT

Once upon a time, there was a problem...

OUR Story

COLLABORATING for RESULTS

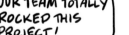

OUR TEAM TOTALLY ROCKED THIS PROJECT!

FRAMESHIFTER meta-ARCHETYPE

UH OH...

SOLUTION!

THINKING
PREPARATION
CAPTURE
SYNTHESIS

DOING
MEETINGS
WORKSHOPS

How to use this book

We have developed a visual roadmap in the spirit of a user's guide to FrameShifting. We begin by introducing you to the archetypes we have encountered. And we encourage you to discover your own archetype, as well as the archetypes that exist on your team, to orient you to the parts that follow.

We have naturally devoted significant attention to framing opportunities and discovering frameworks that align with them. We have devoted equal attention to the behaviors and case studies that illustrate FrameShifting at work. The combination of the more process-oriented skills with the behavioral skills led us to create the meta-archetype of a leader who embodies these principles: the FrameShifter. Regardless of your primary archetype, we have infinite belief that you, too, can learn to become a FrameShifter.

In all of these pages, we want you to embrace the notions of awareness and flexibility as you're working on teams and imagining a better way to collaborate and solve problems. In writing this, we have chosen to be in conversation with you, and the delightful drawings reflect not only our own working styles and personalities, they also serve to make the intellectually sophisticated topic of FrameShifting accessible and hopefully enjoyable to learn.

In his book, *Change by Design*, Tim Brown talks about the nature of design thinking and those who might struggle with the lack of a precise framework and methodology. The key word here is *precise*—the immense potential of design thinking is rooted in the iterative, integrative approach that underlies that framework. Echoing this observation, we are convinced that the complex challenges facing organizations today do not lend themselves to linear and methodical progress. Accepting this truth will help you manage through the inevitable setbacks and turns that are an essential part of breakthrough problem solving. Trust the FrameShifting process, and good things can happen.

Notes

Sketches

Part 2

Meet the Archetypes

pportunity knocks, but it doesn't hang around on the porch waiting for you to get your act together. Whether it presents itself as an emerging market, a potentially transformative technology, or an inefficient process, your challenge is to investigate, size up the situation, and figure out what to do.

There are lots of ways to go about this, and the stakes are high: the speed of change is accelerating, the competition is fierce, and the judgment of the marketplace is swift and brutal. You know that you had better get it right, but how?

Opportunity often comes disguised as a problem, a nagging sense that "this could be better" or "I think we're missing something here." It's a safe bet a thought like this is taunting you now. Maybe that is why you picked up this book. You've read all the other books and tried every trick you could think of. And yet, that one, tangled thing lingers, blocking your path forward. You want to be great—you're stuck at good. You need a better frame.

> **Frame /frām/ (noun): A particular lens for defining an opportunity or looking at a problem or challenge.**

To frame something is to build a box around it, excluding all else, making what is inside the frame the focal point of your attention. Window frames. Door frames. Picture frames. Eyeglass frames. The word itself implies a manageable boundary, simultaneously inclusive and exclusive.

But like facts, problems—or opportunities, if you prefer—are stubborn things. Framing is critical. Ask the wrong question and you will get the wrong answer. Opportunity will elude you. Problems will persist. That is the work of this book and why it is different from the others you may have bypassed on the shelf.

Yet even with a clearly defined frame, solutions don't come easily. You're just getting started. This is where frameworks come into play.

> **Framework /frām wərk/ (noun): A codified way to organize thinking and assess a problem; provides structure and promotes discipline. Specific methods and tools are often linked to the overarching framework.**

A framework is essentially a toolkit for thinking. It provides a set of rules, ideas, or beliefs, often posed as a series of questions designed to help you get to the core of an issue so you can decide what to do about it. The structure of a framework establishes guideposts and offers a problem-solving roadmap, which is critical for working collaboratively with others.

The library shelves are full of excellent books written by knowledgeable experts on this topic, each with a personal approach to "solving for x." Each framework is a specialized tool built for a particular purpose. And, like any tool, it must be properly applied to be effective. That is also the work of this book and why it is different.

FrameShifting is not about promoting a particular framework or approach. It is about the skill of discernment: recognizing when one tool isn't working and how to identify the right one for the job. It is a framework for leveraging frameworks to help you more effectively utilize all of the tools in your problem-solving toolbox.

But, as any good therapist would tell you, before we can fix the problem, we must first understand the people involved. Each of us has our own way of looking at the world. One's perspective is a product of many things, both genetic and environmental. Nonetheless, how we perceive reality has everything to do with how we deal with it—which makes awareness of those around us the perfect place to start our journey.

Over the next pages you will encounter a cast of characters we call "archetypes." Each archetype is viewed through her or his perspective on frameworks. Like all mythical creatures, each is an amalgam of traits and skills, strengths and weaknesses, the full combination of which no one person can possess. Still, blue is blue no matter the subtleties of shade. We recognize the leopard by its spots, and in doing so, we know better how to work with this particular animal.

Each profile describes the archetype's organizational role, skills, and vulnerabilities. You will likely recognize yourself as well as your colleagues in these pages. Take note! To know them is to love them, and you will come to appreciate the gifts each brings to a problem-solving challenge.

The key is knowing how to harness the unique strengths of each archetype in pursuit of breakthrough solutions to thorny problems. This is foundational to the art of FrameShifting. With awareness and patience, you can learn to become a FrameShifter, and we will teach you how.

But we're getting ahead of ourselves. Let's meet the archetypes, shall we?

The FrameMaster

Yves Bellamy is the quintessential Frame-Master. He has spent his career in the automotive industry and is the go-to leader for continuous improvement. After graduating from engineering school, Yves worked in every department in the factory, making his way from managing teams to managing departments to managing the entire plant. After many years he became regional manufacturing director and was on the North American management team.

Yves' lens is continuous improvement. Everywhere he looks he sees endless opportunities to improve quality and efficiency and to reduce costs across the entire value chain of his organization. His framework, of course, is Lean manufacturing.

> **FrameMaster /frām mastər/ (noun): An archetype in organizations focused on one particular framework; has achieved mastery and helps others adopt the framework.**

The role of the FrameMaster

FrameMasters drive framework adoption. They are evangelists for the framework, and they actively seek ways to apply it. People often associate a FrameMaster's role with the framework itself.... He's the *Lean* person, which means others seek his counsel and ask for advice on using the framework.

The FrameMaster's strengths

FrameMasters are exactly that: masters of a particular framework. They are skilled at using it and can help others use it as well. They show tremendous discipline and are adept at applying the framework to new and more complex situations.

In the case of Lean, achievement and teaching go hand in hand. Many practitioners hold a dedicated role and are solely responsible for driving Lean transformation throughout an organization. They understand the organization's culture and how to inculcate new tools. This virtuosity, however, comes with a caveat: exclusivity.

The FrameMaster's Achilles' heel

FrameMasters are usually very loyal to their framework, and rightly so. But that loyalty (and the comfortable familiarity it offers) can prevent the FrameMaster from considering—or even imagining—that any other framework would be as reliable as the one known so well.

Although a FrameMaster like Yves may not realize it consciously, this reality can drive him to force-fit his favored framework into situations where it is stretched beyond its usefulness. The team may consequently feel pressured to use the ill-fitting framework and will become frustrated and stuck because their effort is not producing the desired results.

In the example of Lean manufacturing, practitioners and consultants have been known to advocate Lean thinking as *the* management system to transform an entire organization. Lean in the factory. Lean in the office. Lean in every corner.

Don't misunderstand: Lean is an excellent framework, and Yves can tell you many stories of the productivity improvements that were achieved through Lean tools. But the FrameMaster's colleagues will readily agree that other frameworks are worth learning about to solve very different challenges.

The FrameSeeker

Meet Jan Lathrop. She is known throughout the organization as a thought leader. A voracious reader, she loves learning and hearing about the latest ideas in her industry and the world at large. A lifelong learner, Jan is intentional about seeking ways to expand her horizons through connections outside her organization.

Jan is inspired by innovative FrameBuilders—the big-name consultants and researchers, like Eric Ries and Alexander Osterwalder, who develop new frameworks that spark her curiosity. She follows their Twitter feeds, reads their books, attends the conferences where they are presenting, and networks with her fellow enthusiasts. Her focus is on the people and the thinking behind a new framework, and she gets animated about the possibilities of adopting new ways of working. As you might imagine, TED talks and HBR articles are among Jan's favorite sources of inspiration.

Although her enthusiasm is contagious, Jan is hard to keep up with. She has a tendency to use language and terms that are clear to her but ambiguous or confusing to others. It's tough for her to slow down and help people understand the basis for her interest in a new framework and why it might be relevant. She is generous with handing out books and articles, although her behavior can feel like a never-ending challenge to those who work around her.

> **FrameSeeker /frām sēkər/ (noun): An archetype who avidly reads, attends conferences and events, scanning external resources to find new frameworks and bring them into practice.**

The role of the FrameSeeker

FrameSeekers are connectors. They are the organization's honeybees, venturing to distant meadows for inspiration and returning to the hive flush with new ideas. Like our friend Jan, FrameSeekers understand the organization's challenges and see the potential of new frameworks to drive change. Naturally charismatic and inquisitive, their thinking tends to be ahead of their peers, and they like to share what they're learning. They find joy in introducing consultants and thought leaders to others, and are prone to jump into using a new framework just to try it out. Bring a challenge to a FrameSeeker and she'll probably respond with something like, "Have you read . . . ?" "I think we should try . . ." or "Have you seen . . . ?" It's tempting for team members to get excited and follow the FrameSeeker's lead—the pull of the new and the promise it holds can be irresistible.

The FrameSeeker's strengths

FrameSeekers are full of curiosity and possibilities. They are actively scanning for new ideas and willing to take risks. As lifelong learners, they enjoy experimentation and challenging the status quo. Their intellectual agility gives them the confidence to strike out into new territory with little more than a hypothesis and a roughly drawn map, and their charisma entices others to follow—at least initially.

It's hard to be a stick in the mud with a FrameSeeker around. They are especially valuable to mature organizations that can easily cling to a we've-always-done-it-this-way mindset. FrameSeekers are sure to challenge old ways of working and to push an organization to keep up with a constantly changing world.

The FrameSeeker's Achilles' heel

With all of their intelligence, enthusiasm, and charisma, FrameSeekers are a source of both joy and confusion to their teams. Not only are they known for introducing powerful new ideas and frameworks, they are also known to move on to the next big idea before the current framework takes hold. But "once bitten, twice shy," as the saying goes—this tendency can generate skepticism and concerns about framework abandonment. Having been caught in the FrameSeeker's wake a few times, people are likely to take a wait-and-see approach and avoid jumping on board too quickly.

When encountering a wary team, a FrameSeeker like Jan is likely to observe these types of scenarios:

- The team goes through the motions, as "this too shall pass," and they don't give a new framework a fair shake.

- The team grows frustrated about the source of a new framework and the rationale for using it, using contrarian language and behaviors.

- The team throws the kitchen sink at a problem, hoping to say the right words to impress the boss while never fully realizing the true value of the new framework.

FrameSeekers who experience such situations may press on or give in, depending on the team. Either approach is destined to come up short, and the new framework is off to a discouraging start.

The FrameBuilder

Anita Swanson is a seasoned consultant at a global consulting firm. An expert in customer experience design, she has worked with clients in a variety of industries. Recently, she began working with a new healthcare client, an engagement that offers excellent insight into her framework philosophy.

During her initial analysis, Anita was struck by the complex interactions that existed between patients, their healthcare providers, and their insurance companies. Figuring out a path forward through the labyrinth of processes and requirements would be a heavy lift for a strong, healthy individual. Anita couldn't imagine what it was like under the stress of illness and uncertainty.

In her many years as a consultant, Anita had leveraged multiple customer experience frameworks for clients in other industries. But as she considered each of those options, none seemed quite right for developing strategies in healthcare. Rather than force-fit an existing framework, Anita conducted research and interviews with patients and executives at healthcare organizations. She synthesized the insights and designed a new framework to use with her healthcare client.

Anita's efforts yielded excellent results for both her client and their patients. In fact, the engagement was so successful that she was asked to write a whitepaper that was published on her consulting organization's website. A subsequent HBR case study also featured the healthcare client and the results that the customized framework helped them achieve in their industry. While she appreciated the recognition, Anita was equally pleased to see the new framework implemented and adopted.

> **FrameBuilder /frām bildər/ (noun): An archetype, typically external to an organization, who has considerable skill in a particular problem area and has designed a framework to address it.**

The role of the FrameBuilder

FrameBuilders are innovators and thought leaders who observe emerging challenges in organizations. Often consultants or academics, they view frameworks as the lifeblood of problem solving and critical thinking. Like surgeons, they are methodical and precise in their diagnoses, and they expect nothing less than optimal performance from the frameworks and the tools they employ. Consequently, a FrameBuilder like Anita, who identifies a void in her surgical toolbox, will research and design a new framework to provide the structured thinking and problem solving needed to address a patient's condition. FrameBuilders tend to be experts on a particular problem, and they develop frameworks that support their individual perspective and significant experience.

The FrameBuilder's strengths

FrameBuilders are fearless in their pursuit of excellence. Intellectually agile and creative, they quickly grasp complex concepts and theories, playing them out—like turns on a Rubik's Cube until the colors align—solving for an imagined future state. A FrameBuilder's strong business acumen is often paired with a restless dissatisfaction with the status quo—a powerful combination that fuels their drive to champion a new method of problem solving they believe in.

The FrameBuilder's Achilles' heel

There's a fine line between striving for perfection and obsessing over it, and striking the right balance can be a challenge for FrameBuilders. Their precise nature and ability to create custom tools make them more inclined toward haute couture than to off-the-rack solutions. What begins as a noble pursuit can end up absorbing precious time and resources, with negligible advantage.

And like FrameMasters, FrameBuilders can become wedded to their own frameworks, which may cause them to seek opportunities to showcase the favored frameworks. To the casual observer, it can appear as if the FrameBuilder is trying to sell her solution—a hammer in search of nails, if you will. However, unlike the FrameMaster, whose loyalty to one hammer may blind him to its limitations, the FrameBuilder's toolbox is chockablock with customized hammers, each one precisely engineered to drive a specific type of nail. It is up to expert FrameBuilders like Anita to select the right tool for the job.

The FreeRadical

ree radical is a chemistry term that describes an especially reactive and short-lived molecule, driven (as fate would have it) to find a connection for its unpaired electron. Now, that may sound a bit science-y, but it really is the perfect analogy for this archetype. Smart, curious, optimistic, and contagiously enthusiastic, FreeRadicals are always on the hunt for a challenge. Because they are biased toward action, they are inclined to leap before they look. They are catnip to a problem floating around an organization in search of a solution.

Sarah Mark is a classic FreeRadical. If she were here, she'd tell you that. But, alas, she is off recruiting electrons for a new project. She loves working in the white space, as it were, where she can imagine what might be and put her incredibly creative mind to work figuring out how to bring an idea to life. Now, truth be told, Sarah is not really a framework gal. In fact, she finds structured thinking a bit constraining—thus her attraction to uncharted territory. Not surprisingly, she often quotes her hero, Thomas Edison: "Hell, there are no rules here—we're trying to accomplish something!"

But for Sarah and her team, what begins as a sprint often ends in a frustrating slog. Like a fast-moving river that has breached its banks, they get mired in a swirl of debate and endless meetings with nothing to guide their path forward. It is a cautionary tale for the FreeRadical in each of us—the one who wants to believe that, if we put a few smart people in a room, we can solve this thing! If you find yourself in that room someday, know that a framework might be your only way out.

> FreeRadical /frē ra-di-kəl/ (noun): An archetype within an organization who likes to jump right into problem solving; often a natural brainstormer who prefers unstructured thinking and finds frameworks constraining.

The role of the FreeRadical

FreeRadicals are enthusiastic and collaborative problem solvers. Every company needs at least one in the org chart to push the other molecules out of their comfortable, well-worn orbits and into new, uncharted territory. FreeRadicals are there to ask *why*. They are an invaluable asset to any organization, constitutionally incapable of accepting "we've always done it this way" for an answer.

The FreeRadical's strengths

FreeRadicals are born doers. With their "Bat-Signal" always at the ready, they are quick to gather a team, initiate work, and start getting things done. Happiness is putting check marks in the boxes on their to-do lists. They are most comfortable leading meetings where the planning is around *what* the team needs to do, not *how* it needs to do it.

FreeRadicals like Sarah are naturally attracted to thorny problems, in part because conventional approaches may not have been successful, opening the door for innovation, their home turf. Unencumbered by the constraints of what is, they are free to imagine what might be. That freedom, combined with an enthusiastic "we can do this!" attitude, is often attractive to others with the complementary skill sets needed to bring FreeRadicals' ideas to fruition. And FreeRadicals like nothing more than bringing people together to tackle a tough challenge.

The FreeRadical's Achilles' heel

FreeRadicals are a study in contrasts. They confidently believe in the infinite capacity of human beings to show up committed to any initiative (namely, the FreeRadical's) and have the skills and capability to do great things together. And people will naturally understand problems the same way and won't dawdle about overcomplicating things. Oh, yes—and FreeRadicals also believe that solutions can be quite obvious; and, when the solution is obvious, universal buy-in is a given. FreeRadicals' optimism—dare we say naiveté—encourages a tendency to oversimplify the challenge at hand.

Paradoxically, this bias toward action ends up wasting valuable time and energy. Because "doing" is the FreeRadicals' framework, they jump into solutions too quickly, grabbing the low-hanging fruit and missing the nuances and bigger opportunities that only a deeper, more thoughtful assessment can reveal. In a haste for closure, FreeRadicals may leave others feeling left out of the process, depriving a project of the full benefit of the team's experience and insights. The excitement of working without a framework—*no rules!*—devolves into a frustrating journey without a compass, as meetings meander and multiply in search of progress. Time slips down the rabbit hole along with the team's patience, and the project fizzles out.

Identify your archetype: Take the quiz

You may already have an inkling about your archetype in reading about Yves, Anita, Jan and Sarah. Take this quiz—just three questions—and see if it reveals another side of you. Don't overthink the questions—just select the one answer that best describes you in each of the following scenarios:

1. You've just finished a team meeting that was supposed to end at 5:00 but ran over until 6:30 with no visible progress. Your thoughts as you are on your way home are most likely to be the following:

    a. I need to read up on effective team meetings . . . There must be a better way.

    b. I'm going to share the template we use for team meetings in another part of the company—this team leader could really use some coaching.

    c. Actually, I left the meeting early due to a "previous commitment."

    d. We need to reevaluate why we have these team meetings—we never seem to accomplish anything.

    e. I'm going to work on a new way for us to meet as a team and see if I can get our team leader to agree.

2. Congratulations! You've just been selected to lead an important project for your company. As you're putting together a plan, one of your first activities is the following:

   a. Dig out a recent copy of HBR to locate that really fascinating story about another company's experience working with an esteemed author.

   b. Think about how to leverage a trusted framework for the team to use together.

   c. Start calling bright thinkers and creative colleagues to invite them to your kickoff meeting.

   d. Digest the project challenge and discuss any questions or concerns with your manager.

   e. Begin to think about how to structure the team's work and create a strawman for the team to consider.

3. You've just been offered your choice of Lego sets. Using your instincts, choose the set you would most like to have:

   a. Three of Lego's newest release sets: The average of 800 pieces per set will let you build three different themed creations.

   b. Classic car set: With over 3,000 pieces, you will stretch your Lego building capabilities to the max and have a stunningly detailed version of a classic car.

   c. I'd prefer a set of colored markers and some drawing paper.

   d. It depends . . . Am I building alone or with a partner?

   e. A set of 2,500 individual bricks: No instructions, no manual—just create whatever your imagination envisions.

See the next page for the answer key.

Answer Key

The quiz was meant just for fun, but here is what we would expect from each archetype:

> If you answered mostly "a," you might be a **FrameSeeker.**
>
> If you answered mostly "b," you might be a **FrameMaster.**
>
> If you answered mostly "c," you might be a **FreeRadical.**
>
> If you answered mostly "d," did you read ahead? You might be a **FrameShifter.**
>
> If you answered mostly "e," you might be a **FrameBuilder.**

At this point, you may be feeling confident that you can identify your archetype. Or perhaps you aren't sure exactly, but you've at least narrowed down your options. No worries—these archetypes are designed to help you think about the behaviors that we observe on project teams. And, yes, it's entirely possible to possess multiple archetypes.

If you happen to fall into the "I don't have an archetype" category, don't worry! You are in good company. The fact is, someone who doesn't easily identify with the archetypes is actually the heart and soul of any collaboration: the team player. Perhaps you recognize the archetype behavior in others, if not in yourself. Perhaps you're frustrated by the current state of affairs. Or perhaps you're simply looking for a better way.

Read on, friends.

Notes

Sketches

Part 3

Frame the Problem

> "Our team should have pushed harder for scope alignment from day one. First, we were given a solution, rather than a problem to solve. The project scope changed significantly over the course of the project. For example, the team and its managers clearly thought the project was done in 100 days and became frustrated when it went more than 250 days. In addition, several of the sponsors were not aligned with the idea." —*Rashaad, Innovation team leader*

A successful project has two foundational components: one, a well-framed opportunity or problem statement, and, two, a team that is fully aligned with the defined mission. This epoxy is what holds a project together when the going gets tough. A common assumption by each archetype is that the problem is a given and the team understands the challenge. Unfortunately, this is rarely true. A project in trouble is easy to spot: look for meetings that go on and on, meander down every imaginable bunny trail or swirl in endless debate with no reso-lution in sight. Query the room with a simple question, like "Why are we here?" If no two answers are the same, it's time to check your frame and alignment.

All too often, we find that the problem framed is not actually the problem that will lead to innovative solutions. The temptation to go after the problem you know how to solve—the problem you *want* to solve—is incredibly alluring. Pushing beyond the known takes courage—and skill.

Take, for example, the classic story of Southwest Airlines. While the entire airline industry was focused on the problem of increasing passenger traffic, Southwest made the distinctive choice to focus on making it easier for people driving short distances to fly instead. Why did this distinction matter? Because a different problem drove a different set of solutions.

Another way to look at the Southwest example is from a design thinking perspective and the provocative role of "how might we . . ." questions. The airline industry frame is actually more of a goal than a problem: *increase passenger traffic*. Restating the Southwest frame as a question changes the frame to *How might we . . . make it easier for people driving short distances to fly?* Asking "How might we . . . ?" is such a simple technique, yet it can have enormous consequences.

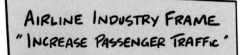

AIRLINE INDUSTRY FRAME "INCREASE PASSENGER TRAFFIC"

ALL FRILLS Airlines

SPECIAL ELITE PLATINUM ONLY! (it's NOT you!)

BOARDING GROUP 12

SOLUTIONS:
- ✓ FREQUENT FLYER PROGRAMS
- ✓ SATURDAY NIGHT STAY DISCOUNTS
- ✓ OFFER AMENITIES: RESERVED SEATS, FOOD, LOUNGES

Southwest ♦ FRAME "MAKE IT EASIER FOR PEOPLE DRIVING SHORT DISTANCES TO FLY INSTEAD"

DETOUR   ROAD CLOSED ☹

SOLUTIONS:
- ✓ FREQUENT ON-TIME DEPARTURES
- ✓ VERY LOW FARES, NO CHANGE FEES
- ✓ NO FRILLS

Framing describes the work of defining a problem or opportunity. The frame establishes the scope of the inquiry and sets the terms of the debate. It is the basis for the central question. It also provides the team's most critical point of alignment: their reason for being.

> **Framing /frāmiNG/ (verb): The activity of developing a frame; can be implicit or explicit depending on the individual.**

The skill of problem framing is so critical that the Yale School of Management dedicates an entire course to it. Yet time and time again we see team leaders minimize this activity or skip it altogether. It is not that they don't value the importance of problem framing. Rather, they assume they know what the problem is, and they accept what has been defined for them by someone else (usually their manager or a senior executive). And even if the team leader has doubts, all too often it's simply easiest to take the path of least resistance. Team leaders treat hypothesis as fact and do not employ a structured process to validate or challenge the assumptions.

When it comes to framing, leaders often trust their gut. Intuition might be a good place to start, but it is a bad place to stop. In Daniel Kahneman's book *Thinking, Fast and Slow*, the distinguished psychologist and Nobel laureate explains the two systems that drive how we think. System 1 is fast, instinctive, and emotional. Its conclusions are based on experience: It tells us what we know based on what we already know. System 2 is slow, deliberative, and logical. It is where we reason and think about what to think about. The key when framing a problem is to use these complementary systems to your advantage. Intuition will tell you where to begin—put you in the right neighborhood, if you will—and an orderly, disciplined framing process will deliver you to the right address.

Regardless of your archetype, when you are asked to lead a team it falls on you to align everyone on a meaningful, well-framed challenge. This is a leadership moment and an opportunity to not only expect but to embrace ambiguity. Your willingness to see gray and resist the appeal of black and white will help you develop an openness to other ways of seeing the problem.

This flexibility is especially important when facing issues for which there is no obvious solution or precedent to follow—issues that are not merely complex or difficult but are fuzzy, hard to define, and beyond the reach of conventional problem-solving techniques. These situations require an entirely different mindset and skill set that we call FrameShifting.

> **FrameShifting /frām SHiftiNG/ (verb): A unique process for looking at problems or opportunities from multiple perspectives to develop a clear, unambiguous frame that can be matched to an appropriate framework; a breakthrough set of activities that transforms "swirl" into productive problem solving that yields innovative solutions. [—FrameShift, —FrameShifted]**

More than a methodology, FrameShifting is a way of being and leading in a "postmodern age," where hierarchy is increasingly obsolete and success depends on a diversity of ideas. It is an active, ongoing process that enables you to assess, adjust, and shape your response in an ever-evolving environment. The principles of FrameShifting apply to everything from how you frame a problem and select a framework to the way you manage your team, share your story, and engage others in your challenge.

By the time you finish this book, you will fully understand the nuances of FrameShifting, as well as the skills needed to be a FrameShifter. First and foremost is the ability to frame a problem—the focus of this chapter. Some people are naturally gifted at framing: They like to think deeply about challenges and are quite skillful at considering other ways of looking at problems. For most people, however, it's not easy to step back and recognize the need to shift one's perspective. Harder still is actually doing it.

If a team is fortunate, their leader is adept at diagnosing when and why they are struggling to make progress, though more often the team simply feels stuck. They know intuitively that they need to shift their perspective and reframe. They want to think bigger and think differently, but they don't know how. So they go back to their "day jobs," vent to others about the team's conflicts and missed timelines, and wonder what to do.

In situations like this, the right tools can make all the difference. Framing is hard work, and there are many ways to do it. To get you started, we have developed three methods that help you and your team evaluate a frame, disperse the fog of uncertainty, and find a new lens for problem solving. Applying these methods is a bit like visiting the optometrist and moving through the various lenses until you find the one that helps you see most clearly. Once a team is fully aligned around a clear, compelling vision, they can embrace their challenge with enthusiasm and commitment. With a unified sense of purpose, the course is set to identify frameworks that are well suited to the challenge.

360° Alignment

Most teams are chartered because someone—often a senior executive—has identified a business challenge or opportunity and has appointed a team leader to organize a cross-functional team to come up with solutions.

The scenario goes something like this: A senior executive hosts an initial meeting to share her thoughts on the challenge as *she* sees it. She also discusses her expectations for the team that will be responsible for developing solutions. Here, the senior executive frames the problem for the team and shares it with the newly appointed team leader.

If you find yourself on the receiving end of one of these challenges, it's important to think about this initial frame as a first draft. Imagine that you are a consultant or advisor: Listen intently to your "client's" frame and then ask penetrating questions. This outsider's perspective makes it easier to resist the temptation to simply run with the ball that's been handed to you. Although framing is a difficult activity and it usually takes longer than anticipated, the payoff is significant. Time invested up front in validating the frame will absolutely save time and resources in the long run.

The 360° Alignment method is a full-circle validation process that captures the individual perspectives of team members who will actually be working together to solve the problem.

Rather than calling everyone together for a kickoff meeting, invite individual team members to meet with you one-on-one to discuss the challenge that has been posed. These more personal conversations will reveal perspectives that are easy to miss in a group setting. During your chat, ask each person for reactions, thoughts, and input on the initial frame. In all likelihood, you will discover conflicting perspectives and additional ideas on how to frame the problem.

Interviewing team members should arm you with new insights and may even give you some homework to do. Gathering additional facts and data may help you reframe the team's challenge into a well-understood statement of purpose. This job of crafting the challenge is best handled by you, as the team leader. *Trust us on this one:* While feedback and input are essential, it is nearly impossible for a team to "group-write" a challenge. Even before the team has its first meeting, you can bring this high-value deliverable to the senior executive, align her on the frame, and reset expectations. With that critical step completed, you are ready to convene the team and share the frame.

Client story: Digital transformation in a manufacturing organization

A manufacturing client decided to launch a digital transformation initiative in the company and appointed Kirk Bingham team leader. Kirk had framed the project with input from the CIO and CEO and invited a cross-functional team to a kickoff meeting. It quickly became clear during that long, fateful gathering that the team members were not on board with the framing presented to them. Instead of focusing on that challenge, participants all talked about what their functional leader expected of digital transformation.

Kirk was frustrated. After all, he had his direction from the CIO. Still, the team persisted in their efforts to reframe the challenge. Kirk decided to restart the initiative with a 360° Alignment. He went back to meet individually with each team member, as well as their functional leaders, to share the initial framing, get their feedback, and better understand their thinking about digital transformation.

Using examples from the team members and their respective leaders, Kirk was able to reframe and clarify the project scope with the CIO. He also made each person feel valued by seeking out and listening to their perspective. In the team's second meeting, he was able to hit the reset button, establish understanding, and build alignment around the project frame, which led to rapid progress in the next phase of the project.

SHIFT FROM
Multiple, competing frames

SHIFT TO
A single, validated frame

The External Flip

We've all been there: The new product launch is underperforming, and the senior executive wants a team to figure out how to hit the revenue target. Pronto!

This is clearly a problem . . . for the company. The issue with defining it as a company problem, however, is that this perspective encourages teams to look backward to try to assess blame or to focus on internal performance fixes. In these situations, companies frequently apply a new-product-launch checklist as their framework for problem solving. While this might yield a few issues or hypotheses, it generally does not produce the breakthrough solutions needed to shift the revenue trajectory into positive territory.

When you see this type of internal framing, it provides a great opportunity to flip the problem. Express it from an external stakeholder's perspective with a simple question: What problem does the customer have? By beginning with an external viewpoint, you avoid the pitfall of chasing the symptoms that fail to understand the real problem or opportunity—a FrameShift that will yield far better solutions.

Client story: Financial issues at a mental health provider

Lori Kelley, CEO of a mental healthcare nonprofit, was under enormous pressure. After several stellar years of building client programs and making huge improvements in key quality metrics, the nonprofit's board raised the stakes. Several local healthcare systems were providing funds to offset financial losses incurred from serving underinsured or uninsured clients, and the board wanted Lori's organization to operate at breakeven or better.

Lori's business challenge was clear: She needed a team to devise a fiscally sustainable strategy for serving underinsured/uninsured clients. Unfortunately, while the organization had a healthy stream of donations and grants, additional fundraising was not expected to make up the shortfall.

Her team was uninspired and frankly at a loss. Their slow progress clearly indicated that they had no idea where to begin. One board member pulled Lori aside and suggested design thinking as a method to help break the log jam. The team embraced the idea of empathy interviews and began talking with clients about their hopes, wishes, and fears. Their learnings and insights helped them identify several opportunities to serve clients in new ways with new sources of revenue.

Instead of viewing the problem through an internal, financial lens, the team posed a customer-focused question: "How might we help clients after they leave our offices?" This new frame felt true to the nonprofit's purpose and enabled them to tap into a much deeper well of innovative solutions. The team turned a corner. Brainstorming was prolific, and prototypes were quickly developed.

SHIFT FROM
A challenge the organization is facing

SHIFT TO
A challenge the customer is facing

Discovery Session

The Discovery Session is designed especially for the FreeRadical archetype. It provides a FrameShifting mindset while satisfying the FreeRadical's innate desire to "dive right in." Assuming that the problem at hand is framed sufficiently well enough to inspire solutions, the Discovery Session lets you test your frame to see how it plays using a familiar, tried-and-true framework. Instead of diving headfirst into the deep end of problem solving, this method lets the team dip its collective toes in the water first. No commitment required, just a nice, safe place to start—for even the most skeptical swimmers.

Truthfully, we don't love this method. The risk is that it combines framing and frameworks, making it difficult to assess the frame independently. Yet experience has taught us that teams love to get started—even the other archetypes—so we developed the Discovery Session.

With this caveat in mind, select a familiar framework (one that you know well and feel comfortable using) to see how the frame plays out. Be disciplined about using the framework in this process. Invite potential team members to attend one meeting—a Discovery Session—and observe the pace and energy of the discussion. Remember that you're testing your frame with a known framework; it doesn't have to be perfect. If you're on target, the meeting should feel like you're on the right track.

This structured approach is a simple one, with a low investment of time, to assess your hypothesis and validate your intuition. During the session, look for solutions that feel relevant. The discussion should be lively and energizing. You may even discover ways to affirm your initial path. If so, congratulations!

If things don't go so well, analyze the conversations held during the Discovery Session and try to understand what the team members were struggling with and what questions they posed. Hopefully, valuable insights will arise to help you reframe the problem. Thank the team for participating in the Discovery Session, synthesize what you learned, and consider using 360° Alignment or External Flip to finalize the frame. With a solid foundation in place, you're ready to reengage the team with a project plan and move forward with confidence.

Client story: Debating new product development at a global organization

Steve Rankin led a small niche business at a global organization. Though the business was highly profitable, it was always viewed as an adjacency and somewhat in competition with the core business. Sales leadership had identified ways to grow the business by expanding the customer base, but they needed new products, and the CEO was not on board with their plan.

Steve brought his business team together to talk about how to persuade the CEO of the plan's logic and rationale. They talked about how important these customers were and why it made sense to invest in solutions for them. The team decided to use a business model framework and focus on the strategic choice of which customers to serve in what markets.

After a robust discussion, a member of the team asked an interesting question. She wanted to know the CEO's mindset about this niche business in relation to the core business: What did success look like for him? Her question led to a breakthrough for the team, changing their perspective from "where to play" (Steve's customer target perspective) to "how a niche business contributes to or detracts from the core" (the CEO's financial perspective).

This new frame shifted the team's position from defense to offense. Using a framework that reflected their symbiotic relationship with the core, they were able to highlight their past financial contributions—a very compelling and profitable story. This shift was a game changer and made it possible for them to find a solution that everyone, including the CEO, could agree to. Steve became an evangelist for framing, telling others, "At first, I really didn't know where this was going. Then, suddenly, it became clear. I was blown away by the power of changing our frame."

SHIFT FROM	SHIFT TO
Your own perspective and how to get buy-in	Listening to another perspective and discovering a new path

In closing

*F*raming is a discrete, essential step in the problem-solving process, and it is vital to inspiring brainstorming and innovation. If you're getting great results, you likely have a great frame. If the process is a grind and results are weak or nonexistent, it's a signal that the frame may be flawed.

There are, of course, many ways to frame a problem or opportunity. The key to effective framing is aligning a team around a meaningful challenge. Launching a project with a team that is unclear on the reason it exists is like trying to shoot a movie without a script. In order to play their parts well, all of the actors need to be on the same page. An aligned team both understands and agrees with the frame. In other words, a great frame inspires your team to put their best efforts forward because they know that their work matters.

Here are a few ways you will know you're working with a powerful frame:

☑ Everyone can name the frame.

Ask anyone on your project team to describe the "it"—the thing they're working on. If you consistently get the same concise description of the framed problem or opportunity, you've nailed it. When everyone is on the same page, they will respond with energy and excitement. (If not, you'll know they haven't bought into their mission; people are pretty transparent).

"We're trying to figure out how to make plastic bottles a thing of the past!"—*Blueland*

☑ People don't confuse a project name with an opportunity frame.

A great frame transcends the project itself. Teams can't wait to share the frame so that others can offer insights and support the team's efforts. However, when you hear excited conversations about the new "it" project but nobody can explain exactly what "it" is, look out! This lack of clarity is the precursor of scope creep and timeline delays. Worse yet, team members on poorly framed projects will sometimes craft a definition that best suits their narrative, thereby wasting time and energy on extraneous solutions.

"We're working on Project Amazing, but I'm really hoping we'll tackle what I think is amazing." —*Individual who has a pet solution in search of a problem*

☑ Storytelling is rich and is told by a larger circle.

Senior executives, team leaders, and team members talk about the frame as if they discovered a treasure. People actively engaged in defining a powerful frame find as much joy in telling the story of their journey of discovery—how the team found the opportunity—as they do in talking about the results they achieved. These true believers make the best evangelists for the cause, because they are personally invested in the frame and are proud of their role in identifying a compelling challenge.

"Fall in love with the problem, not the solution."
—*Innovation adage*

☑ There is energy when the frame evolves over time.

Framing is rarely a one-and-done activity. Working on difficult problems often leads to discoveries that cause the team to revisit and reframe as they learn. An engaged team will embrace change as a natural part of a healthy process—unlike so-called "normal" teams that wish they could just stick to their knitting . . . and (sigh) *"Here we go again . . ."*

"We thought we were headed in the right direction until our intern showed up and asked the most phenomenal question! It revolutionized our perspective, and our new frame has the possibility to be a real game changer." —*Veteran team member*

Notes

Sketches

Part 4

Select the Framework

We hope that the layered meaning of FrameShifting is becoming clear to you by now. In Part 2, we introduced you to the archetypes as a way to understand yourself and those around you. In Part 3 we discussed the concept of framing, including some of our favorite methods to help you shift your perspective to frame a meaningful problem. Now it's time to talk about frameworks—the tools that will help you generate solutions to solve the problem at hand.

As the world we live in becomes more complex, so do the problems we encounter. Solving for these specialized, multifaceted challenges requires the diverse talents and input of a team, rather than a lone individual. Each member of the team brings a unique perspective, experience, and skills to the challenge. The success of the endeavor depends on the ability to collaborate— and collaboration doesn't happen by simply scheduling a meeting and gathering a bunch of people in a conference room. It takes work to build unity. In fact, it's built right into the word: col-*labor*-ate!

Collaborate /kə- la-bə- rāt/ *(verb)*: To work jointly with others or together, especially in an intellectual endeavor. [From the Latin: col (together) + laborare (to work)]

Creating a collaborative environment requires you to think about *how* the team will work together. There are two elements here: emotional intelligence and the nature of the work itself. There are several excellent models to help develop healthy team relationships and team norms. We like, for example, the Myers-Briggs Type Indicator (MBTI) and Herrmann Whole Brain Thinking. We encourage you to consider these and similar tools

to boost your collaboration efforts—they can be quite useful in helping you understand individual preferences and styles and can provide practical methods for adapting how you work with others.

FrameShifting is focused on structuring the team's *actual work*—their labor, if you will. Whereas MBTI helps you understand the sixteen personality types to foster more productive interaction, the FrameShifting methodology is about shifting them into action. It helps you diagnose and frame meaningful challenges and choose or adapt an appropriate framework to solve them. In some sense, it's like an MBTI for wicked problems!

As we said in Part 3, framing is the inspiration for solving a problem—the first step. And this frame drives the next step: the selection of the framework. The job decides the tool, not the other way around. All too often, however, we find that the archetypes choose a framework based on personal preference, not on its fitness for the challenge. This explains, at least in part, why so many frameworks fall in and out of favor, are abandoned altogether, or never take root in an organization. From the team's perspective, this cycle leads to skepticism and trepidation about learning new approaches. It also results in a problem-solving toolbox that is poorly curated and not particularly useful.

The good news is that it doesn't have to be this way. In Part 4, we share our thoughts on the power of frameworks and provide methods for choosing and using frameworks that fit the opportunity you've framed.

Frames, frameworks, and structured thinking

We are strong advocates of the importance of frameworks—when they are paired with a powerful frame and applied intelligently to the challenge at hand. To understand why, it's worth taking a moment to explain our rationale for structured thinking and the role that frames and frameworks play in streamlining the path toward innovative solutions.

Structure is critical in motivating teams to get to work on the real business of problem solving. Although the human mind is capable of its most creative and innovative work when left to its own devices (dreaming, sleeping—unfocused and unstructured), the vast majority of work in organizations requires, and benefits from, collaboration with others. In his book *Powers of Two*, author and essayist Joshua Wolf Shenk asserts that partnership—not lone genius—is the real driver of human creativity. When it comes to getting big things done, two heads are indeed better than one.

Working with others isn't always easy, though. As we learned from our archetypes, everyone has a unique way of thinking—and this can lead to differences of opinion, to say the least. Frameworks reduce the friction between competing approaches by laying out a disciplined structure—defining a path, if you will—that is incredibly useful in helping the team move forward. By providing a means for "thinking about thinking," frameworks help the team figure out how to go about the work of working together—how to structure their work—so they don't get lost in the fog of competing ideas about where to start, where to go next, and how to focus on solving the problem at hand.

While it is common to hear that structure stifles creativity, the overwhelming evidence and our own experience suggests the opposite. Structure is the guiding force of creativity. Structure helps us organize our work into manageable, solvable chunks. Structure enables us to identify and exclude the extraneous and nonessential so that we can focus on the important. The sonnet imposes its restraint on the poet, not the subject. In his essay "Poetry and Marriage," writer Wendell Berry reminds us that "the impeded stream is the one that sings."

Frameworks are the riverbanks of a creative endeavor, providing direction, flow, and velocity. Nobody understood this better than David Ogilvy. Known as the father of advertising, he famously insisted, "Give me the freedom of a tight brief!" No, he wasn't talking about underpants; he was stressing the critical link between structure and creativity. In the advertising world, the creative brief integrates the frame and the framework—organizing the thinking of the client and the agency to align the two teams.

Recall that Sarah, our FreeRadical, is not a big fan of frameworks, generally speaking. Those who identify with her archetype may be reflecting on their own "adrift at sea" team experiences. Jumping into problem solving without a framework is like setting sail on a ship without a rudder: When your destiny is known only to the wind, the crew grows restless and the threat of mutiny is always nigh.

In what now seems like the very distant past, people came to work to perform the repetitive tasks that, increasingly, have been replaced by technology. In today's workplace, being able to think creatively and work collaboratively are highly sought-after skills. We are entering what the economist Klaus Schwab calls the "Fourth Industrial Revolution," and those looking to future-proof their skills need to be adept at complex problem solving, critical thinking, and creativity.

"The future of work is creative, meaning work is about solving increasingly complex problems in new ways."
—*Amy, VP Strategy*

But complex problem solving, critical thinking, and creativity are not easy skills to develop. And it can be frustrating and downright annoying when leaders ask people to "think differently" or "think outside of the box" as if it were all about attitude. If someone is thinking inside the box, they're probably not even aware of what that box is or why they're inside it. So if you want your team to think differently, show them how!

Fortunately, there is a continually evolving set of thinking methods and tools to support people asked to deal with these complex problems, and team leaders can benefit from seeking out and learning about relevant frameworks. In 1993, Bain & Company began surveying executives around the world about the management tools they use and how effectively those tools have performed. Their objective: to provide managers with information they need to identify and integrate tools that will improve bottom-line results and to understand how global executives view their strategic challenges and priorities.

Frameworks are a consultant's stock in trade, and they can be a fantastic resource for leaders and teams. But you do not have to be a consultant to adopt the discipline of finding and using frameworks with higher frequency and effectiveness. In fact, the pain points experienced in typical problem-solving environments may make using frameworks even more imperative for those who are not consultants.

In the late 1990s, the Michelin company was running an iconic advertising campaign. It featured a baby sitting in a tire, along with the famous tagline "Because so much is riding on your tires." The ads helped sell a lot of products, especially to older, more conservative drivers who associated Michelin with safety. Every planning season, the advertising agency was challenged to find ways to breathe new life into the campaign and align with the marketing calendar of promotions, product launches and events. Their frame was all about keeping the baby campaign fresh with product news.

Meanwhile, the marketing strategy was beginning to change. A new customer segmentation framework was helping the marketing team identify growth opportunities among different groups of tire buyers. Their findings indicated that the baby campaign, though memorable, was not impactful across all customer segments. One important group of customers still loved it, but they were getting older and buying fewer tires. A larger—and growing—target market of younger, more performance-oriented customers was simply not as interested in the family responsibility story.

The data from the customer segmentation framework made the response clear: The advertising frame had to change. Michelin challenged a new ad agency to create a message that would resonate with younger tire buyers, which the agency did. A brand-new campaign was launched, and sales increased dramatically as younger consumers switched to Michelin. Reframing the advertising challenge led to a period of unprecedented growth and profitability in the business.

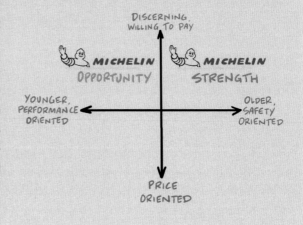

SHIFT FROM	**SHIFT TO**
Framing based on "the way we've always done it"	Leveraging a framework to provide new insights to reframe the challenge

Take note of the interdependencies of frames and frameworks that may send you backward to propel you forward.

Discovering and choosing frameworks

The very act of deciding to choose and use a framework for your challenge is critical to success. Once you've committed to using frameworks as an essential part of structuring your team's work, you will soon realize that you have no shortage of options to choose from. Curiosity about frameworks in general leads to experimentation, which invites assessment. Our FrameSeeker, Jan, does this naturally, and the rest of us can learn from her skills.

Adopting a mindset of experimentation will help you find the frameworks that work . . . for *you*. Your curiosity also will connect you with other people who have experimented and assessed frameworks that might be new to you. Taking a page from Jan, it's possible to find joy in this discovery phase, bringing consultants and thought leaders into the conversation as you decide how to structure the team's work.

Keep in mind that you are building your framework toolkit. Like any toolkit, it will contain your reliable favorites, as well as a few specialized instruments tucked away for a specific purpose. With experience, you will become adept at matching the framework to the challenge. You will learn their strengths and limitations. You will also find newer, fresher tools to replace old, worn standbys that don't work as well as they used to.

Assessing a framework, after all, is really about appropriateness or fit and, ultimately, of utility. Did the framework fulfill its role? Did it help organize your thinking? Did it help assess the problem? Did it provide structure and discipline?

Remember, the goal is not to have the biggest toolkit; you want to have the right tools for the types of challenges you encounter. A pipe wrench is of little use to a carpenter, and there is no benefit to carrying extra baggage. As you approach a challenge, think carefully about what role the framed challenge plays in your organization. Consider these scenarios when introducing a new framework:

- **The frame is new or is not well established within your team or company.**
  Your challenge is to develop a holistic customer experience strategy, but the company's current customer journey is an amalgamation of discrete touch points developed independently over time. This is a perfect moment to find a handful of alternative frameworks and explore using them with a small team.

- **The frame has multiple legs and occurs frequently.**

  Disruptive trends, such as the digital transformation of activities and business processes, may warrant learning new frameworks. A brief Google search will reveal a myriad of options, testament to the desire (and need) for a relevant set of tools to help address increasingly complex technologies. In this situation it may be wise to appoint a FrameMaster to benchmark other companies and lead the introduction of a new set of tools with a potentially large number of users.

- **The frame occurs infrequently.**

  It's seldom wise to invest in learning a framework that may not be used on a regular basis. Mergers and acquisitions, for example, require specialized expertise, which can be extremely costly in both money and time. If M&A is a rare activity for your company, you may be better off inviting external consultants with significant experience and methodologies to work with you.

- **The frame is unique to your organization.**

  Framing is not always about finding and applying an existing framework—sometimes you need to build something from scratch. It may be that you need to develop or access the skills of a FrameBuilder, like Anita. Someone at your organization with deep expertise in the challenge may be capable of building a custom structured framework.

Of course, it's always good to have a "generalist" tool on hand, one that the team has lots of experience with and readily accepts. Learning and adopting a new framework—perfect as it may be—consumes precious time and energy. And, when introduced too quickly, it can fail for the wrong reasons.

It's often better to take an 80% approach and use a "good enough" framework that can be leveraged easily. Business model frameworks are a case in point: There are many different frameworks that serve essentially the same purpose. A review of published frameworks reveals that consultants and academics more often agree than disagree on elements of a business model. The 80% approach would favor finding the model that resonates with you and sticking with it.

Here are a few takeaways from our archetypes to keep in mind as you think about frameworks and their effectiveness:

Yves, our FrameMaster, advises that "a tool is only as good as the person's skill at using it." It's easy to underestimate the learning curve with a new framework, and it's also easy to confuse familiarity with experience. Let's look at SWOT analysis—an old favorite for many and an easy framework to get started with.

Most anyone familiar with SWOT analysis will tell you they understand that it is a strategic planning framework for identifying strengths, weaknesses, opportunities, and threats. A significant proportion of these people will confess that they are not entirely sure how to differentiate these four aspects, so they often just try to complete the framework to finish the process. There are also a few bold souls who will admit believing that SWOT is a tired and not very useful framework.

At first glance, the framework seems pretty simple. So why do so many people struggle with it? Albert S. Humphrey, one of the creators of SWOT at SRI International, explained the framework this way:

> SWOT analysis came from research funded by the Fortune 500 companies to find out what had gone wrong with corporate planning and to create a new system for managing change. We started as the first step by asking, "What's good and bad about the operation?" Then we asked, "What is good and bad about the present and the future?" What is good in the present is Satisfactory, good in the future is an Opportunity; bad in the present is a Fault, and bad in the future is a Threat. Hence S-O-F-T. This was later changed to SWOT—don't ask.
>
> Following the analysis step, we sorted the issues into six programme-planning categories of: product, process, customer, distribution, finance, and administration. By sorting the SWOT issues into the six planning categories, one can delineate short- and long-term priorities. This approach captures the collective agreement and commitment of those who will ultimately have to do the work of meeting the objectives. The planning process was developed into a seventeen-step process beginning with SWOT.

Wow—if you're like us, you're probably thinking, "Apparently, I don't know SWOT!" How could anyone get great results from this framework outside of its intended context and without the support of the seventeen-step process?

On the other hand, an elementary SWOT analysis can be a very useful, open-ended analysis that bridges to another planning process. This approach can work especially well with teams who are not strategy experts, because it elicits and incorporates their observations and insights as valuable input. Sometimes good is good enough, and simplicity beats perfection.

SHIFT FROM
Making assumptions about skill with a given framework

SHIFT TO
Taking explicit steps to build common ground

Our FrameBuilder, Anita, cautions against "framework myopia" and the pitfalls of choosing a framework for situations that it was never designed to address. Familiarity can motivate us to keep testing a framework's usefulness, simply because it is hard to find and learn a new one. Consultants, motivated to expand a business that is deeply vested in a particular framework, may be inclined to encourage this tendency. Caveat emptor.

The business world offers notable examples of good frameworks gone rogue. Michael Cusumano's 1994 article in the *MIT Sloan Management Review* foretold "The Limits of Lean." As more and more companies embraced the mantle of continuous improvement, he worried that Lean was creating a future environment of parity.

> *This parity will make it necessary for all firms to seek competitive advantage not simply by following the Lean principles that everyone will know and be implementing, but by defining other domains of competition, such as new levels of manufacturing automation, new materials and technologies, innovative product features, or skillful overseas management and expansion into developing markets.*

More recently, the Agile framework is an emerging example of this phenomenon of stretching a framework beyond its limits. In 2016, the *Harvard Business Review* published "Embracing Agile," an article positioning the methodology, which was initially designed for software development, as a framework for innovation. Two years later the magazine trumpeted "Agile at Scale," promoting this once specialized tool as a universal framework. Agile quickly became a buzzword as teams everywhere tried to force-fit it onto their pet projects. Sadly (perhaps cynically), we could have predicted the next HBR headline, which appeared in 2020: "The Agile C-Suite."

What do these three articles have in common? A "framework first" approach advocated by FrameMasters and FrameBuilders. To be clear, this doesn't make the authors or their frameworks problematic. On the contrary, these passionate, persuasive evangelists bring great things into the world. No, the problem, to paraphrase the famous Pogo cartoon, is us—the unquestioning followers.

Instead of climbing on the latest bandwagon, a savvy team must determine a framework's fitness for the challenge they have framed. This calls for a healthy dose of skepticism and due diligence. Resist the temptation of a "universal framework" and proceed thoughtfully.

SHIFT FROM	**SHIFT TO**
Overreliance on a particular framework beyond its intent	Determining a framework's fitness for the challenge in front of you

If you're a FrameSeeker like Jan, take a look at the frameworks you already have before you go searching for something new. We've said it before, but it bears repeating: The cost of abandoning a well-understood framework is significant. It takes significant time for a team or an organization to learn, accept, and build proficiency with a new tool. Unless the case for change is well documented and compelling, the switch can also cause unnecessary confusion, leaving team members to wonder why their favorite tool is no longer valued.

The SWOT analysis is just one of many good frameworks that were adopted but are no longer in use. Remember Michael Treacy and the three value disciplines of Operational Excellence, Product Leaders, and Customer Intimacy? How about Jim Collins and his framework that included First Who . . . Then What and The Hedgehog Concept? Just because a framework has been around a while doesn't mean it isn't useful. Collins recently released a monograph on The Flywheel Effect, and it has a renewed following. This deceptively simple framework helps you identify your economic engine and find ways to accelerate momentum. In other words, it's very possible for a framework to find tremendous value today despite being published nearly twenty years ago.

Whether you have a tendency to cling to the familiar or abandon the unpopular, we encourage you to be thoughtful and intentional about your choices. Be prepared to slow down and be fully immersed in a potential framework to appreciate its utility and appropriateness for your situation. As one client said, "I can tell when the thinking is good." There's a feeling of satisfaction when a team is collaborating well and moving forward with energy and commitment. You'll know it when it happens!

SHIFT FROM	**SHIFT TO**
Gravitating too quickly towards newly popular frameworks	Weighing the costs of abandoning proven frameworks

Introducing and applying frameworks

*f*ramework discovery and selection are certainly important. We also believe that, in order to achieve lasting success, you should invest equal care and attention in *how* you introduce a framework to your team, as well as to broader audiences across your organization.

Our FrameSeeker Jan, in particular, often encounters skepticism from her colleagues when introducing a new framework. *("Oh no, here comes a new framework to complicate our lives!")* The reaction has two contributing factors: the frequency with which Jan finds and tries to apply new frameworks, and her tendency to underestimate the difficulty of the buy-in process.

While their methods can sometimes be frustrating, FrameSeekers play a valuable role in the organization: They bring diversity to the problem-solving toolkit. Without FrameSeekers like Jan, teams are inclined to keep hammering away when what they really need is a screwdriver. To help Jan and other FrameSeekers, we've developed a few guidelines for introducing and sharing new frameworks, based on well-established principles of change management.

- **Set aside a specific event to introduce the framework to others.**
  Tell the story of how you learned about the framework and why it seems relevant to your challenge. Encourage people to become familiar with the framework by sharing relevant books, articles, and white papers or attending training events. It is also helpful to discuss why other existing frameworks weren't selected.

- **Be willing to struggle with a new framework.**
  We've discussed a few reasons why a framework might not be working, including a very common one: lack of skill in using it. Don't bail when the going gets tough: *trust the process* long enough to make a fair assessment. Likewise, when you think you need to shift to another approach: *trust your instincts.* When human beings come together to collaborate, anything can happen! Remember, FrameShifting is not only about being willing to shift the frame, it's also about being willing to shift the framework.

- **Let the framework provide the structure for sharing your solutions.**
  Involving people outside of your work team is a great way to begin sowing the seeds of framework adoption across the organization. As you socialize the project team's challenge and alternative solutions, it is also a great opportunity to share the team's journey of choosing and

using the framework. Storytelling is so important to FrameShifting that we have dedicated an entire chapter to it in Part 5 of this book. *Hint: if you're encouraging your team to think differently, learn to harness the power of visual communication!*

- **Enlist a FrameMaster like Yves to partner with you on a new framework.**
A FrameMaster is an invaluable partner in helping you and your team move beyond the superficial to achieve a deep understanding of the framework and build the skills to apply it successfully. Someone like Yves will likely jump at the opportunity to attend a webinar, read a book, or meet with the followers of a new framework. And if he's fortunate enough to connect with the FrameBuilder, like Anita, their synergy will yield benefits in abundance.

In closing

Framing and frameworks go hand in hand. This might seem obvious, but the reality is that the two are often disconnected, ill-defined, or even absent from collaborative endeavors. Anchored by a good frame and an aligned team, a framework that is designed for the challenge sets the course for achieving great results.

So you may be wondering . . . Where is our "top ten list" of frameworks? (But you are probably not wondering why a "top ten list" of frames is missing from this book.) The answer relates to relevancy. Framing is a very specific activity that provides a meaningful challenge to a specific team and a specific organization. It follows that the frameworks  that will be most useful to you are inextricably linked to your frames. We resist the idea that there are certain frameworks that "everyone" should know and use (even though there might be a few worthy of strong consideration).

Team members who are reading this can undoubtedly relate to our story about Agile reaching the C-suite. It's all too common for an organization to decide to roll out a major initiative to learn a new framework. When disconnected from a well-framed challenge, the framework is a training initiative without a target. Imagine that the prerequisite for learning about a new framework—learning that is both relevant and timed with the point of need—is to identify the problem you're hoping to solve and that a skilled set of FrameMasters could introduce you to the appropriate framework and tools.

FrameShifting is about bringing a flexible mindset and a disciplined approach to the intelligent use of frameworks. We're hoping to heighten your awareness of two factors simultaneously: the act of framing and the discipline of frameworks. This awareness will serve you well as you think about thinking in your next challenge. FrameShifting is about a leadership mindset, not about a specific set of tools. While the methodology is universal, your toolbox—your trusted companion—belongs to you.

And don't underestimate the importance of a framework sketched on a napkin. You may be feeling that finding frameworks is a mountainous task. Yet people have done amazing things by sitting across a table from a colleague and thinking about how to approach a problem. As the

2020 COVID-19 pandemic began to unfold, and on the same day that the coronavirus pandemic was declared a national emergency, a storied New Mexico hospital established the nation's first drive-through testing for the virus. How did they figure it out? On a pair of napkins.

This low-resolution approach also works with team meetings: The basic elements of structuring a team's work can be accomplished with collaboration agendas. An agenda that is organized by discussion topics and timeframes is the norm. An agenda that is organized by outlining exactly how the team will be working together to address each topic is a very different sort of meeting. You can do this by putting on a FrameBuilder hat and thinking about structuring the team's work.

Allan Chochinov, chair of the MFA in Products of Design at the School of Visual Arts, had this to say about knowing when something is right: "It was perfect. It was so simple. And it was obvious. That's how designers know that they have the 'right' solution, by the way—when that solution seems completely obvious . . . after the fact, of course!"

The right framework can activate this same experience—that "knowing feeling" is an unmistakable indicator that you're working with a powerful framework. Here are a few more signals that tell you you're on the right path:

FRAMEWORK CHECK

☑ **Your team can describe the framework.**
When you're leading a team that can describe their challenge, you're off to an excellent start. When the same team can also explicitly reference and discuss the framework employed, they're owning the collaboration process with you. Successful collaborations are sources of energy and inspiration to others. Listening to how people talk about the work will reveal the true level of alignment.

☑ **Working sessions are focused and productive.**
The combination of a great frame and a powerful framework will significantly increase the team's productivity. You will likely notice a mood shift that is openly optimistic, especially if the team is tackling a challenge that has stymied others in the past. This optimism, along with the feeling of time well spent, is contagious. In addition to being committed to the team's

work, each team member will also be contributing at a higher level. This collective, focused effort is what produces breakthrough results.

☑ **There is an uptick in meetings ending on time and deadlines being achieved.**
Not only do frameworks help organize thinking, they also contribute to a sense of closure as the methods and tools provide guardrails and boundaries. At the start of a project, there may be an initial warming-up period as team members buy into the framework and accept it as a path they agree to follow. Yet once the team hits their stride, the structure of a framework helps them "begin with the end in mind." You may not be able to see the solution, but you can envision how you are going to get there. You learn to trust the process.

☑ **And, most importantly, the solutions are relevant, innovative, and inspiring.**
Isn't this the point, after all? FrameShifting is about equipping you with skills to meet wicked challenges head-on. By that standard, the ultimate test of a great framework is the results you achieve. Understanding the archetypes, learning to frame, and working with appropriate frameworks: they're all in the service of collaborating for better results. To echo an earlier client comment: You'll know when the thinking is good.

Notes

Sketches

Part 5

Storytelling with Impact

We have written in great detail about the FrameShifting methodology: what it is, how it can transform an organization, and how to develop one's skills. But this treatise would be remiss in failing to highlight the art of storytelling and the pivotal role stories play in a project's success.

Why do we love stories? Storytelling is an ancient and essential human activity. Stories help us process our experiences and share them with others. Fundamentally, a good story harmonizes the factual with the emotional, connecting the worlds of head and heart. A good story is universal, reaching us at a deep, personal level to activate a sense of purpose.

Neuroscientist Paul Zak has conducted research showing that good stories actually increase the oxytocin levels in our brain, because they kindle feelings of empathy with others. He found that "character-driven stories with emotional content result in a better understanding of the key points a speaker wishes to make and enable better recall of these points weeks later. In terms of making impact, this blows the standard PowerPoint presentation to bits."

For most organizations, the central character is the client or the customer. When you put the customer at the center of your story—showing their challenges and struggles, and the solutions you envision to help them—you are imagining a better future. This is a classic story arc. It is the type of story that is likely to trigger the kinds of emotional, and literally chemical, responses that will get your team bought into the idea that the company must act and make people in the organization more inclined to help.

Crafting a story

The very act of constructing a story forces you to dig down deep to answer very basic questions: So what? Why does this matter? How does this affect the listener? In a memorable TED talk, Oscar-winning film director/screenwriter Andrew Stanton offered one rule for a great story: *Make me care.*

This edict is as relevant in business as it is for Stanton and his team at Pixar. As with framing and framework selection, constructing and sharing a story takes time, attention, and discipline. Not a one-and-done activity, it is an ongoing and integral part of a successful project, providing a vital forum for engaging stakeholders, team members, and the organization at large. In addition to testing your thinking from multiple perspectives, each conversation becomes a node in a network of navigational buoys that help you shape and, when necessary, adjust your charted course.

Powerful stories share a few basic tenets. As you craft and prepare to share your story, ask yourself the following questions:

Why are you telling this story?

Whether you are sharing the story of your framing journey, the framework you selected, or the possible solutions you have identified, your goal is to invite feedback. You are engaging in a conversation, not a one-way presentation. So be prepared to do more asking and listening than telling. In addition to the basic facts of the story, you should also provide context to help the listener understand why you chose a particular path—as Simon Sinek said, understanding "the why" behind an idea is the prerequisite for buy-in. Together with Stanton's advice, it creates a useful equation for a powerful story: Tell me why = make me care.

Who is your target audience?

You will probably have several audiences that you need to engage, especially if you are working on a complex or cross-functional project. To help identify and prioritize these groups, draw a series of concentric circles. Place the name of your project sponsor in the center, and work your way outward to create a solar system of stakeholders, implementers, and influencers. In addition to your sponsor, select a small group of people from this list to be your "thinking test market." As your project matures, you can expand your communication to larger audiences.

What are the key facts the audience must understand or accept?

This is all about ruthless editing. Of all the things you have to say, what are the three or four most critical for your audience to hear? Focus on this content first and keep any supporting information as backup. If you are proposing several options for consideration, be sure to include pros and cons, assumptions and/or constraints for each possibility—be ready to show your work, so that the audience has the information they need to provide helpful feedback. This approach will ensure that your message is clear and your bases are covered.

What is the call to action?

What do you need/want the listener to *think, feel, or do* with the information you are sharing? Everything in your conversation should build to "the ask." Be explicit about what you need from the audience. Whether you are recommending a specific option or need input to help sort out the best among several solutions, make sure that you clearly state your perspective and expectations.

Making your story visual

Words are powerful, but images speak volumes all their own; put the two together and you can achieve something magical. Humans are visual creatures; our brains recognize images thousands of times faster than text. Even the simplest, most rudimentary drawing can help clarify an abstract concept. Counterintuitively, less is more when it comes to this type of imagery. It's not about art, it's about communicating ideas. Artistic detail and flourishes distract the viewer's attention from what is important. So keep it simple, and choose your images carefully. Each picture should serve as a visual bullet point that triggers a fuller, more nuanced story in the viewer's mind.

A SIMPLE CIRCLE IS AN EASY WAY TO DEMONSTRATE THE HUMAN BRAIN'S PREFERENCE FOR VISUAL INFORMATION.

READ IT → "A PLANE FIGURE BOUNDED BY A CURVED LINE, EVERY POINT OF WHICH IS EQUALLY DISTANT FROM THE CENTER." FUNK & WAGNALLS

Hmmmmm...

HEY! NOBODY SAID THERE WOULD BE A MATH QUIZ!

SOLVE IT → $X^2 + y^2 = r^2$

WHICH CIRCLE IS EASIEST FOR YOU TO RECOGNIZE?

SEE IT! BING! →

Sharing stories

Strategist Roger Martin encourages project leaders to share their work with key stakeholders early and often. Rather than waiting until a solution is etched in stone, Martin suggests constructing a series of interactions designed to elicit constructive feedback on critical elements of your project, including framing, possible solutions, and the assumptions and constraints you've identified. This cycle of co-creative continuous improvement not only helps shape and improve the thinking, it broadens and strengthens support for the outcomes.

One of our clients, Judy, has a useful model for eliciting feedback that you may want to employ. Before prototyping a solution, she drafts a short list of smart people she thinks will give her good advice and help her connect to others' thinking. This is her "thinking test market." As she meets with each person, she often draws her idea on a whiteboard so they can "see what she's saying." Judy's simple drawings invite interaction and feedback because they feel more malleable—unlike formal slide decks or highly polished digital content, which can make an idea seem more fully baked than it actually is. This produces far better results than the typical didactic, show-and-tell presentation.

Stories make information accessible and infinitely shareable. The job of the storyteller is to translate complex, even abstract, concepts into a clear, concise, actionable narrative. Here again, your FrameShifting skills will serve you well. Tools like the External Flip, which we shared in Part 3, will help you develop an analogy—maybe an allegory or a simple picture—that engages and activates your audience. Together, this strategic combination of words and pictures will make even hard data more palatable and memorable.

> **Client story: Challenging an operations team to imagine and build a future state**
>
> A large manufacturing company found itself in an increasingly competitive business. The market was changing rapidly, and the executive team was looking for new ways to create value. To shake things up a bit, the CIO agreed to take on a new role as VP of Global Operations. As an IT guy, he looked at the organization with fresh eyes and wondered how the company might better leverage data and technology to create strategic advantage. He chose the delivery experience—that rather underappreciated segment of the customer journey between order entry and receipt of the product—as his initial target.

Manufacturing, by nature and necessity, is a culture very focused on the here and now. Their job is to "make the donuts," and their frame emphasizes safety, quality, cost, and efficiency. The new VP's challenge was to unlock his organization's creativity and enable them to transcend their literal, numbers-driven world to imagine a future state beyond the shipping dock, where anticipating and receiving a product could be a market differentiator. He selected a seasoned team leader, and together they devised an unconventional approach.

The VP and the new team leader convened a small team to meet with customers, mine the data for insights, and facilitate a series of cross-functional workshops to explore opportunities for innovation. All pretty normal stuff, but with one small twist: They invited a designer from the communications group to help the team visualize their ideas. The invitation proved to be a pivotal decision. With paper, markers, and a bit of imagination, the designer helped the team express solutions and experiences that did not yet exist, stitching them together in a storyboard that enabled the team to easily share its vision. The story sparked imaginations across the company, initiating a movement that transformed virtually every aspect of the delivery experience—from packaging and loading to the role of the truck driver. Today, they are using this storytelling approach to tackle other segments of the customer journey, delighting everyone involved.

SHIFT FROM
Overemphasizing logic, facts and data

SHIFT TO
Balancing logic and emotion with visual storytelling

Notes

Sketches

Part 6

The FrameShifter Meta-Archetype

*I*n a very broad sense, problem solving is the process of eliminating the gap between a desired outcome and what actually happens. By that definition, it is fair to say that this activity absorbs much of an organization's time and energy. Yet unless you work in a consulting firm—which is a unique, FrameBuilder type of culture—there is typically no function or role in an organization responsible for the intelligent use of frameworks and framing methods, even though both are critical to achieving successful outcomes.

The irony is that we are sentient, thinking beings living in an action-oriented culture. To the outside observer, the act of thinking may appear passive—don't just stand there, do something! But a thoughtful pause is worth its "wait" in gold. In fact, military strategist John Boyd made it the first step in his OODA Loop decision-making framework for military operations: Observe, Orient, Decide, Act. Notice the process begins with attentive awareness and ends with action—not the other way around.

The truth is most people don't "think about thinking" very much, especially when it comes to problem solving. Instead, they tend to fall in love with a particular approach and use it over and over without taking the time to observe its impact or efficacy. Did the approach make the difference we expected in our priorities and results? A lack of critical awareness also applies to our archetype. For the most part, we move through our day unaware of the unconscious decisions that motivate behavior—our own, as well as other people's—until that reality is brought to our attention.

Perhaps you recognized some of the skills and Achilles' heels we described in "Meet the Archetypes." If so, you are beginning to develop the attributes of a FrameShifter—the meta-archetype in our cast of characters who has developed the situational, social, and self-awareness that is key to the FrameShifting methodology.

FrameShifters strive to align their teams in a way that continually seeks common ground, transforming conflict and meandering debates into constructive dialogues. FrameShifting is an auxiliary skill set that can be learned and practiced, whether you see yourself as a FrameMaster, FrameSeeker, FrameBuilder, or FreeRadical. In this part, we share insights on each archetype and, in doing so, hopefully inspire you to begin your own FrameShifting journey.

Meet the FrameShifter

The FrameShifter is a critical thinker who brings intentional objectivity to the framing process. When exploring a problem, she has trained herself to set aside her biases and look beyond the obvious. This healthy detachment enables her to shift her perspective and examine a situation from multiple viewpoints.

The FrameShifter's ability to reframe opens the path to breakthrough problem solving. By shifting into action with the *appropriate framework*, she can guide teams to collaborate effectively and deliver results in far less time than is true of typical projects. She understands the challenges of each archetype and is skilled at bringing out their specific strengths. She doesn't direct the action; rather, she creates an open and inviting team environment, sharing stories with others and illuminating the path forward by visualizing solutions.

> **FrameShifter /frām SHiftər/ (noun): A leadership meta-archetype that embraces the philosophies and mindset of FrameShifting. Alert and aware, uses FrameShifting methods to discover powerful frames and collaborate with other archetypes to structure problem solving with the best-fit framework.**

The role of the FrameShifter

The FrameShifter is a transformational leader who achieves breakthrough results by adapting and applying frameworks with intelligence and savvy. She recognizes and deeply appreciates the key skills of the other archetypes. She knows how to leverage the collective strengths of the archetypes, enabling them to work far more effectively together than on their own.

The FrameShifter's strengths

The FrameShifter is excellent at framing problems and opportunities. Laser-focused on getting results, she can cut through the fog and get to the core of an issue quickly. She also possesses a healthy level of skepticism that is fundamental to her ability to suspend judgment and shift her perspective, when needed. Flexible and adaptable, she enjoys learning from others and understands how best to leverage each person's expertise and skills. But the bow on top of this prodigious skill set is her storytelling mastery. She knows that a solution—no matter how wonderful—has little chance of being implemented if it is not well understood. However, a well-crafted story shared in an environment that invites feedback is a powerful way to improve even the most innovative of ideas.

The FrameShifter's Achilles' heel

It's possible for each archetype to acquire the skills of a FrameShifter. But, like all skills, they require learning and practice. One of the keys to success is objectivity: the ability to step back from a situation and make a clear-eyed assessment about where you are, how you got there, and what it will take to move forward. That is not easy to do, especially under pressure.

Consider Sarah Mark; her primary archetype is a FreeRadical. Under stress, she is apt to revert to her default setting and "dive in!" Her impulse to quickly get results is always lurking in the background, which can tempt her to overrule her better judgment. This revert-to-type behavior can happen to any archetype.

The important thing is that Sarah is aware of her tendencies. So, when she gets the urge to run toward the diving board, she knows to stop, put on her FrameShifting hat, and assess the situation. Is the framework working? Does the team just need a push? Or is it time to try a different approach?

It is vital to understand that the goal of becoming a FrameShifter is not to stop being a FreeRadical, FrameBuilder, FrameMaster, or FrameSeeker. Far from it! The unique attributes of your archetype are what make you so valuable to your company and your team. Think of FrameShifting as an added superpower that lets you objectively assess a situation, properly frame—or reframe—the problem, and chart a path forward.

Becoming a FrameShifter

The FreeRadical: Sarah's Story

Sarah Mark is an intuitive leader who, in her early career, led with enthusiasm and a can-do attitude. A FreeRadical at heart, Sarah is always ready to dive in and get things moving; her optimism is contagious. Yet as her responsibilities changed and expectations grew, she began to notice that things weren't going so well. Unfortunately, she tended to find herself leading teams stuck in the swirl of debate and struggling to move beyond the idea stage. Meetings were interminably long; deadlines were postponed. Amidst these dark days, implementation often seemed like a far-off dream.

Sarah's "aha" moment

In a particularly memorable encounter, as Sarah prepared to kick off a new company initiative, a senior executive named David invited her to coffee. A former consultant, David wanted to know Sarah's framework for structuring the project. She replied that her team deeply understood the opportunity frame and was anxious to get started. They needed space for brainstorming, and a framework might hold them back. David gently challenged Sarah's FreeRadical approach, suggesting that brainstorming alone might not be good enough for such a complex initiative. He knew from experience that, without a framework, team members and stakeholders were unlikely to understand and buy in to possible solutions.

David caught Sarah at a vulnerable moment; she actually was a bit worried about how to lead the new initiative successfully. In fact, it was precisely Sarah's desire to become a better leader and contribute at a higher level that made her open to his counsel. With coaching and mentoring from David and others, she was inspired by the power of frameworks and began her transformation into a FrameShifter.

Now, instead of staying stuck or bailing on her team, Sarah, though still a FreeRadical, takes a different path. Perhaps more than any of the other archetypes, this is a significant departure from her instinctive behavior. In the midst of the fog, she is willing to step outside her comfort zone and face hard truths, shift her perspective on the problem, and embrace a FrameShifting approach.

Now think about that for a moment. Consider how hard it is to change course once you've started down a path, especially when others are looking to you for answers. You can probably hear the chorus: "You're the leader! What do you mean we've been rowing in the wrong direction?! All our work is wasted!"

Over time, however, Sarah developed expertise on an arsenal of frameworks, giving her the confidence and flexibility to select the one that best suits the opportunity frame—choosing the right tool for the job makes the work a lot easier. Today, her intellectual closet is well organized, and that clarity helps her remain calm in a turbulent environment. She is truly a FrameShifter.

The FreeRadical's growth areas

FreeRadicals are a powerful force. Their ability to inspire and motivate a team is unmatched. In order to harness that energy, however, they must master the counterintuitive discipline of slowing down to speed up. While it may be tempting to turn loose the horses and watch them run, the project is better served by a unified team pulling in the same direction.

This cohesiveness can be achieved only by taking the time to frame the problem, choose a framework, and align the team on how the work will be done. Although Sarah initially resisted its constraints, she learned quickly that a framework provides the structure and discipline needed to formulate an effective solution. With this foundation in place, the team can shift into action and sustain its momentum throughout the project. As checkmarks fill the boxes and the team delivers results, the FreeRadical can enjoy the true benefit of FrameShifting: the reward of a job well done.

SHIFT FROM		**SHIFT TO**
Leading with personal energy and drive	>	Harnessing the team's energy through structure and discipline

The FrameMaster: Yves' story

Our colleague Yves is one of the most trusted leaders we know—and for good reason. As a FrameMaster, he was pivotal in his company's understanding of the power of structured thinking, helping them achieve extraordinary results from Lean frameworks and tools. Largely dedicated to challenges framed by the operations and logistics teams, Yves yearned to see the rest of the organization embrace Lean. He decided to actively try to recruit a few disciples to help replicate his work in other functional areas.

Yves' "aha" moment

Yves set up a meeting with Sheryl, the head of marketing, to talk about Lean and how to introduce it to the marketing team. Sheryl listened to Yves' rationale and, although she wanted to be open to new ways of working, she was concerned. Frankly, she didn't see any similarity between the challenges in marketing and the types of issues an operations team would encounter. How would Lean improve marketing effectiveness?

Yves was almost ready to admit defeat when he asked Sheryl if there was any area in marketing that was particularly slow and cumbersome. This piqued her interest. "Yes!" she said. The new product development process took several years, and it would be fantastic to shorten the time to market. Specifically, marketing felt stymied by the engineering and R&D teams and their "overly rigid" approach. Yet the marketing team didn't know how to change the situation. Could Lean help with this?

Although Yves didn't fully realize it yet, he had just stumbled on the absolute necessity of framing a challenge before introducing a framework. The challenge from Sheryl gave him his first glimmer of what it would take to become a FrameShifter: he needed to rethink his "framework-first" approach.

The FrameMaster's growth areas

By developing their FrameShifting skills, FrameMasters will both increase their breadth of knowledge and expand their sphere of influence. This means moving beyond an attachment to a single framework and diversifying the toolkit. For Yves, the journey is about increasing his focus on framing and resisting the assumption that his go-to framework will fit. This journey won't be an easy one for him to take. He's spent years mastering his framework and is continually searching for ways to apply it. But, as his conversation with Sheryl suggests, intellectual curiosity is an essential component of his journey.

By exposing himself to new frameworks, Yves will develop new mental models for understanding the relationship between a particular framework and the specific types of problems for which it is suited. Gradually, he will become more and more framework agnostic and flexible in his approach. He will also escape the pigeonhole of a one-framework ideology.

In essence, FrameMasters become multilingual. As with their native tongues, FrameMasters tend to be most comfortable with their original framework and apt to try that first. But, over time, as they expand their repertoire and increase their fluency, they experience the benefits of flexibility and a growing sphere of influence. This positive reinforcement accelerates their transformation as a FrameShifter. No matter where they find themselves, they can quickly translate their approach to the language of the challenge—a powerful skill indeed.

SHIFT FROM
Being wedded to (and typecast with) a single framework

SHIFT TO
Increasing attention to framing and seeking out alternative frameworks

The FrameSeeker: Jan's story

Recall that Jan is our FrameSeeker: intellectually curious and a student of life. With abundant charm and many diverse interests, she is the perfect dinner guest and conversationalist. Her MBTI type would most likely include P for perceiving, as she is always absorbing new information, though she is not quite as oriented to decision-making. Jan relies on her reputation as someone continually providing external perspectives to drive her career trajectory. She relies heavily on those around her to take inspiration from her FrameSeeker behavior and most often finds herself as a valued team member, but rarely a team leader.

Jan's "aha" moment

Jan had been at the same job in the same company for a number of years and was, frankly, ready for a change. She applied for several different positions but was not selected for any of them. This confused Jan; she knew people genuinely appreciated her skills, because they regularly invited her to work with them. In some sense, her well-known "healthy dissatisfaction with the status quo" made her a go-to team member.

Frustrated, Jan decided to ask for some feedback and guidance from Cho, a manager she respected. He confirmed that indeed Jan was a great team member and that people, himself included, valued her contributions. But Cho also confided a difficult truth Jan needed to hear: while she was absolutely valued for her ideas and intellect, she had trouble sticking with projects over the long run. Ever the seeker, she tended to move on to the next interesting challenge, leaving others to do the heavy lifting that is needed to deliver results. If Jan wanted to become a team leader, she would need to demonstrate that she could drive positive outcomes.

Cho's gift of constructive feedback motivated Jan to look for opportunities to partner with others known for their ability to deliver results, focusing her attention on things she hadn't noticed before: How, for example, these people framed a challenge, introduced frameworks, and shared solutions as stories. True to her nature, she channeled her love of learning and became a student of FrameShifting.

The FrameSeeker's growth areas

FrameSeekers need to be thoughtful and intentional when deciding to share a new framework with an organization. They must think beyond the framework's initial appeal—often simply the fact that it's new—to consider the unique value this fresh approach provides. To become FrameShifters, FrameSeekers must understand how the new framework will help address a team's specific challenge. For Jan, this enables her to clearly articulate the case for change within a context her colleagues can embrace.

FrameSeekers also increase their impact by considering frameworks that are in an organization's existing toolkit. The case for change may not always carry the day when the goal is to select an appropriate framework for the problem.

FrameSeekers also are wise to enlist the help of FrameMasters, who bring depth and tenacity to the challenge of inculcating any new approach. Together, FrameSeekers and FrameMasters can craft a plan to build awareness for the new framework and develop the skills needed to successfully apply it. Becoming adept at introducing and piloting new frameworks will help FrameSeekers pave the way for mastery and adoption across the wider organization.

SHIFT FROM	SHIFT TO
Assuming the team will share a desire for new and different ways of working	Bringing the team along with their thinking, and being willing to change course

The FrameBuilder: Anita's story

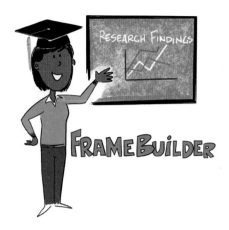

Anita Swanson, our FrameBuilder, is a supersmart woman who excels at studying, learning, and undertaking all manner of intellectual pursuits. After earning her MBA at a prestigious university, she joined a consulting firm where she was surrounded by other bright, motivated, and curious individuals. Anita loved the problem-solving environment, where the possibilities were endless and practicalities mere footnotes. As Anita began to handle repeat engagements with clients, however, she noticed that progress was slow, or worse yet, nonexistent. She wondered why all the great thinking, brilliant frameworks, and skilled analysis produced such meager results. Although she was disappointed, Anita wasn't sure what to do.

Anita's "aha" moment

After a full-day client work session, Anita noticed that one of the participants, Kami, was clearly frustrated. Throughout the day, Kami had been reluctant to participate, peppering Anita with questions that signaled discontent with the planned process. Anita decided to meet with Kami after the workshop, hoping to smooth things over.

As they began talking about the day and about Kami's struggles at various points, Kami said something that both intrigued and surprised Anita. Direct and to the point, Kami cut to the chase. "I just don't understand the framework you're using; it doesn't make sense to me. I need to understand where you're going to see how I can contribute."

Roberto, another workshop participant, was shutting down his computer and couldn't help but overhear the conversation between Anita and Kami. He admitted to Anita that he was in the exact same boat. She agreed to meet with them early the next morning to discuss the framework.

Despite the early hour, the trio had a powerful, thought-provoking conversation about the development of the framework and the purpose of its various elements. Kami and Roberto asked probing, insightful questions and challenged Anita in ways that made her step back and really think about what they were telling her. It was a pivotal moment in her development as a FrameShifter.

Thanks to their feedback, Anita gained a deeper appreciation for the importance of properly introducing a client to a new framework. By not taking the time to on-board and align the entire team with the frame and the framework, she inadvertently excluded valuable contributions from key players, thus limiting the constituency of any proposed solutions. Without the full support of the team, these ideas would likely languish on the pages of the presentation deck she delivered at the end of the engagement.

Lesson learned, Anita also came to appreciate that her clients could not only master the frameworks she developed, they could make them even better. After all, they were living the framed challenges every day, and they had a much deeper understanding of their company's situation than an outside consultant ever could. In a lovely twist of fate, becoming a FrameShifter had the additional benefit of making Anita a better FrameBuilder!

The FrameBuilder's growth areas

FrameBuilders need to appreciate the importance of properly introducing a groundbreaking framework to the people who will be using it. Taking a page from design thinking, Anita developed empathy, which helped her better understand where the team members were struggling. Without understanding, there is no alignment. And without alignment, there is little chance for collaboration.

And then there is the issue of pride of ownership. To avoid the perfectionist's trap, the FrameBuilders must learn to fall in love with the problem—better yet, the opportunity it presents—instead of falling in love with their framework. As we said at the onset of our journey, the framework provides guidelines and boundaries—a set of rules, ideas, or beliefs to help you get to the heart of the matter to be addressed. Often the "perfect" framework is a subtle twist on an existing framework. Relinquishing the familiar may not be worth the imagined benefit. Frameworks needn't be perfect to be effective.

When the goal is to get the job done, it's essential to take care with each part of the process. FrameBuilders are wise to remember that recognition comes in many forms, but none so powerful as seeing their vision embraced and successfully implemented.

SHIFT FROM
Focusing on the intellectual framework attributes

SHIFT TO
Developing empathy and respect for the individuals involved on teams

FrameShifters and organizational impact

FrameShifters embrace FrameShifting as a powerful leadership skill set. They understand that high-performing organizations need better ways to collaborate and innovate. Learning to FrameShift equips leaders and teams to solve wicked problems and exploit growth opportunities that resist traditional ways of working.

Collaboration is not easy to do under the best of circumstances. Opinions differ. Passions flare. In order for the team to move forward, the conversation must focus on the principle rather than the personal. The FrameShifting lexicon provides a common language—a framework, if you will—for navigating difficult conversations by defining precisely what is meant and what's expected.

This common understanding facilitates the exchange of ideas. It provides the foundation for building a FrameShifting culture—one that recognizes the value of each individual's role in the organization and of their skills, challenges, and opportunities for growth. This language also helps foster an environment of mutual respect that is essential to unlocking the full potential of a diverse team.

At this point, it's important to reiterate the complementary relationship between the skill sets of a FrameShifter and one's core archetype. FrameShifting skills enhance individual strengths; they don't replace them. The FrameShifter is a "meta-archetype" who possesses superpowers that undergird all archetypes (think "yes/and," not "either/or").

In the universe of superheroes, the dynamic duo is far more effective than a lone warrior. As you develop as a FrameShifter, consider partnering with other archetypes to help you increase your effectiveness. As you move from being a novice to a seasoned FrameShifter, you will begin to acquire skills of the other archetypes: mastering, building, and seeking out frameworks.

The FrameMaster

Highly trusted for discipline and framework mastery, a FrameMaster is an excellent ally when introducing a new framework to an organization, especially for addressing unprecedented challenges and complex situations.

The FrameBuilder

The FrameBuilder is an ideal coach and mentor for the FrameMaster, sharing expertise and perspective on a specific opportunity area to help inculcate a new framework.

The FrameSeeker

The FrameSeeker is a great source of knowledge for a new FrameShifter who can, in turn, help extend the FrameSeeker's influence across an organization.

The FreeRadical

Uncharted territory is the FreeRadical's happy place. Include a FreeRadical on a project that is testing out a new framework and let her or his can-do attitude inspire the team.

As you can see, the Frameshifting methodology enables the different archetypes to work in harmony, engaging and leveraging the collective power of their individual strengths. Once a team is working together in a true col-*labor*-ation, they become an unstoppable machine that can roll with the changes and adapt to whatever the future may hold.

Troubleshooting guide

Despite every good intention and explicitly embracing FrameShifting, sometimes things just don't go as planned. Understanding the principles is one thing; applying them is another, and becoming expert is a lifelong journey.

Carissa Carter, at Stanford's d.school, uses the analogy of cooking to talk about mastery. She compares a cook to a chef: *"The order and process of a recipe helps new cooks get started, but it's only with practice, inventiveness, experimentation, and constraints that you might begin to call yourself a chef."*

When you're not making the progress you had hoped, it's time to reinforce the FrameShifter objectivity lens and assess the situation. We've put together a short list of possible warning signs and common pitfalls to look out for and some suggestions to help you move forward.

- **The "boss effect"**

  It happens to all of us—when the boss stakes out a position, it's not easy to remain objective. This can happen at any part of the process. It might be the boss is locked on a particular frame. More commonly the boss is locked on a particular solution. And, yes, bosses are quite often inflexible on project timelines that might be forcing shortcuts that hinder alignment.

  When the "boss effect" happens, it is much easier to diagnose in the rearview mirror. When you're in the moment it's tough to think like a FrameShifter—let's face it, we all want to make "the boss" happy. We encourage you to make a habit of taking some time to think before heading in a particular direction—whether driven by the boss or even by another strong-willed individual on your team. Asking for time to "sleep on it" is a thoughtful response to someone who is committed to a position.

  Situations like this also demonstrate why it is hard to be a solo FrameShifter in an organization. To see the real impact of FrameShifting, bring "the boss" and your teammates along in your leadership journey. Begin to use the FrameShifting lexicon to gently remind others of the purpose of aligning everyone on solving a meaningful challenge and structuring the team's work.

- ## Beware the long scope document

  "If I had more time, I would have written a shorter letter." Often attributed to Mark Twain, this witty truism originated from French mathematician and philosopher Blaise Pascal.

  A project leader once shared the scope document for an initiative he was asked to lead. It was four pages long and 1,750 words. There was actually a concise frame near the bottom of the first page, but the project leader pulled from other parts of the document to explain the challenge. And that muddied the waters quite a bit.

  You may feel that a short, crisp frame benefits from context and expectations. That can certainly be true. It's just too easy for the context and expectations to overshadow the frame. If you decide to write a scope document—or edit it—make sure the framed challenge is up front and in bold. In journalism speak, don't bury the lede.

  And keep the scope document to one page, following the storied example of P&G's "one-page memo" discipline for key documents. Depending on people to read four pages of context is leaving much to chance. One of "Murphy's Laws" of communication from Finnish researcher Osmo Wiio: "The more communication there is, the more difficult it is for communication to succeed." This law is not about the frequency of the message—it's about the length.

- ## Framework fatigue

  Team dynamics are influenced by so many different things, and a FrameShifter needs to be constantly aware of the team's mood and energy level. When using the structure of a framework, there are times when the group will get bogged down. People crave rules and boundaries, yet they want to do things their own way. Maybe the group needs a wellness break or an energizer. Maybe they need to try a different approach.

  It can also be helpful to give the group some latitude as they're losing steam with a given framework. Be willing to give the team the freedom to adapt or deviate from the framework. Sometimes this "permission" is just what a team needs to riff a little and regain momentum. And you can return to the structure if and when the group seems ready.

  You may also find that it's actually the team leader who can propose an alternate method or tool as a way to reinvigorate the team. Role-play can be a great way to get active and get people engaged again. Stand up, take on a persona, and start the improv. Whatever it takes, be willing to adjust your plans.

- **The "room where it happens"**

  Okay, this is a sneaky way to pull in a quote from Lin-Manuel Miranda's *Hamilton*. But isn't it the truth? Who is in the room where it happens?

  If your team is stuck, or swirling, or having disputes, or revisiting tired solutions, you may need to think about the players on your team. In Lean methods, there is a strong preference for having people closest to the work solve the problems. In innovation it's the opposite. Radical collaboration means inviting people who have vastly different experiences and bring diversity to the team. Inviting just one new player to the team—and sometimes providing an exit to another—can change the dynamics quickly and profoundly. Don't be reluctant to shift the team members.

  And speaking of the room, consider the following. Is the room a space that fosters collaboration? Does it have natural light, flexible furnishings, and tools that support active participation? It's easy to underestimate the impact of "the room where it happens."

Remember that a key tenet of FrameShifting is being aware and being flexible. There is no definitive rulebook for FrameShifting—our methods and experiences are simply guidelines. They provide a way for you to get started and to be more intentional about how you collaborate. We absolutely encourage you to ideate, prototype, and test new ways of FrameShifting—asking "how might we" questions that propel you to work better together.

Notes

Sketches

Part 7

Collaborating for Results

t's not easy to learn new ways of working. Yet it's far harder to navigate today's problems using yesterday's roadmaps or flying by the seat of your pants. These default behaviors consume valuable time and energy with little to show for the efforts.

Nearly any endeavor depends on collaboration to thrive. It takes work to build unity. As we have pointed out, it's built right into the word: col-*labor*-ate! In these pages of *FrameShifting*, we have shared our process for structured thinking that aligns teams on the challenges that matter and the frameworks that fit them. Forgive our word play, but FrameShifting proposes a concrete path to "take the labor out of collaboration."

Underlying the principles and methods of FrameShifting is a philosophy about humans. We believe in the innate capabilities of humans to do amazing things. But those pesky humans will make half-hearted contributions or derail projects if they are not on board. The essence of FrameShifting is fundamentally about harnessing talent and bringing out the best in people.

When you become a FrameShifter, you have a heightened awareness of each person on the team and their primary archetype. You're continually seeking common ground to align your team members and inspire their best work. And when you notice that someone is struggling, you're willing to shift your perspective and find another way.

Does FrameShifting always work? Perhaps surprisingly, the answer is yes, although reframing and pivoting consume time, energy, and quite a bit of patience. In our experience, a general rule of thumb for a team leader is 4:1 "thinking" to "doing." Half of the thinking ratio (2:1) is about preparing for a working session; the other half (2:1) is about capturing and synthesizing content from a working session. And this "thinking" is what makes the "doing" so productive for a FrameShifter's team.

So, yes, FrameShifting works—if you can make the time and you have the fortitude and discipline to follow through. At the beginning you will need to learn to trust the process. As you and others in your organization gain skills, it will become easier over time.

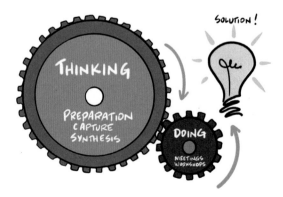

A few key points to remember:

- A successful project has two foundational components: a well-framed opportunity or problem statement and a team that is fully aligned with the mission.

- Framing is the inspiration for solving a problem—the first step. And this frame drives the next step: the selection of the framework. The job decides the tool, not the other way around.

- Frameworks help the team figure out how to go about the work of working together—how to structure their work—so that they don't get lost in the fog of competing ideas about where to start, where to go next, and how to focus on solving the problem at hand.

- Storytelling—particularly visual storytelling—is unmatched at building alignment and inviting feedback. Logic may be the basis for the story, but the story is what captures imagination.

- FrameShifting brings a flexible mindset and a disciplined approach to the intelligent use of frameworks. Framing plus frameworks. A heightened awareness of two things simultaneously: the act of framing and the structure of frameworks. This awareness is a leadership mindset of a FrameShifter.

The individual team player perspective: When individuals work together in a true collaboration, it's fun and rewarding. There's no doubt that each of us can recall a time when that happened, and it's unforgettable. That this happens so rarely is regrettable, and yet it doesn't have to be this way. Give someone a meaningful problem and a fully committed team, and watch as they rise to the challenge.

The senior executive perspective: Collaboration and innovation are at the top of any CEO's list of desired skills in the workplace. Understanding and applying the FrameShifting methodology develops a breakthrough capability that is essential to solving wicked problems and exploiting market opportunities. FrameShifting expertise translates into tangible impacts that bring about sustainable value creation—the ultimate scorecard.

The FrameShifter perspective: As a FrameShifter, you are always learning. Shifting your perspective on others and understanding archetypes. Shifting your perspective on problems and framing meaningful challenges. Shifting your perspective on structured thinking and linking frameworks to the frame. As we were writing this book, it happened to us. Writing a book was a new challenge, and we needed a framework for our writing partnership. We drew upon insights from other writers, and when we got stuck we improvised with a back-of-the-napkin framework.

It's made our collaboration a labor of love.

Notes

Sketches

Notes and Resources

The archetypes and characters in this book are intentionally fictitious, although their stories and behaviors have been inspired by real clients we have known. Our purpose is to have these stories demonstrate the principles and methods of FrameShifting rather than to focus on specific case studies. Out of the highest regard we have chosen to respect the confidentiality and privacy of the people involved.

Two exceptions have been made: Alison's experience at Accenture and at Michelin. These personal stories were instrumental in forming her perspective on frameworks.

Introduction

- The conversation over coffee at Accenture was with Yaarit Silverstone and David Andrews in San Francisco. Anil Swami, also a partner at Accenture, introduced Alison to them during the customer transformation engagement at one of Accenture's largest clients in the utility industry.

- Philip Kotler describes the four "Ps" of the marketing mix in *Marketing Management: Analysis, Planning and Control* (Prentice-Hall, 1967, with multiple updated editions).

- Michael Porter describes the Five Forces in industry competition in *Competitive Strategy: Techniques for Analyzing Industries and Competitors* (The Free Press, 1980).

- The Boston Consulting Group framework can be found at https://www.bcg.com/en-us/about/our-history/growth-share-matrix.

Part 1

- When Jim Hackett was CEO at Steelcase, he introduced Alison to design thinking and gave her a stack of books to ponder. Among these was Tim Brown's *Change by Design: How Design Thinking Transforms Organizations and Inspires Innovation* (Harper Collins, 2009).

Part 2

- For reading about Lean manufacturing, one of Alison's favorite Lean practitioners, Jeff Hebbard, recommends two books from Pascal Dennis:

- *Andy & Me: Crisis & Transformation on the Lean Journey* (Productivity Press, 2nd ed., 2010).

  - *Lean Production Simplified: A Plain-Language Guide to the World's Most Powerful Production System* (Productivity Press, 3rd ed., 2015).

- One of Alison's go-to guides on innovation is Eric Ries' *The Lean Startup: How Today's Entrepreneurs Use Continuous Innovation to Create Radically Successful Businesses* (Crown Business, 2011).

- The most comprehensive work on business model innovation, *Business Model Generation* (Wiley, 2010), was written by Alexander Osterwalder and Yves Pigneur and co-created by "an amazing crowd of 470 practitioners from 45 countries."

- "Don't ask what? Ask why?" is a key tenet of design thinking, also found in Tim Brown's *Change by Design*.

Part 3

- Roger Martin has written extensively on strategy. His 2011 paper "A Background on Strategy" is fantastic, although unfortunately not in circulation. In it he shares his thinking on strategic choice architecture, including where to play and how to win. The paper also presents a great visual of Southwest Airlines and their activity system. For a publication still in circulation, try one of the other books Jim Hackett gave to Alison: *The Design of Business* (Harvard Business School Publishing, 2009).

- "How might we …" questions are explored in a design thinking method card found in Stanford's d.school bootleg (https://dschool.stanford.edu/resources/design-thinking-bootleg), or you could enroll in the Stanford Bootcamp and learn it from the experts in Palo Alto (https://dschool.stanford.edu/programs/executive-education).

- Yale School of Management's Problem Framing course is taught by Paul Bracken (https://som.yale.edu/elective-core-courses).

- Daniel Kahneman, *Thinking, Fast and Slow* (Farrar, Straus and Giroux, 2011).

- Mitch McCrimmon does a nice job defining postmodern leadership in his blog post "Leadership in a Postmodern Age" (https://www.lead2xl.com/leadership-in-a-postmodern-age).

- Blueland is advancing the idea of eliminating single-use plastic bottles, and their mission is extraordinary (www.blueland.com).

Part 4

- The Myers-Briggs Type Indicator (MBTI®) can be found at www.myersbriggs.org.

- Ned Herrmann's Whole Brain® Thinking is described at www.thinkherrmann.com.

- Joshua Wolf Shenk, *Powers of Two: Finding the Essence of Innovation in Creative Pairs* (Eamon Dolan/Houghton Mifflin Harcourt, 2014).

- Wendell Berry, "Poetry and Marriage" (*CoEvolution Quarterly*, Winter 1982).

- Klaus Schwab, founder and chairman of The World Economic Forum, *The Fourth Industrial Revolution* (Currency, 2017).

- Bain & Company, "Management Tools and Trends" (https://www.bain.com/insights/topics/management-tools-and-trends/).

- It's hard to overstate the significance of working with a ground-breaking customer segmentation framework to transform marketing for the portfolio of brands at Michelin. Alison worked with Scott Clark and Sheryl Henderson to develop marketing strategies that enabled decision-making and results that were previously unattainable.

- SRI International Alumni Association, December 2005 newsletter (https://archive.sri.com/about/alumni/alumni-newletters).

- Michael A. Cusumano, The Limits of Lean (*MIT Sloan Management Review*, Summer 1994).

- Michael Treacy and Fred Wiersema describe the three value disciplines in *The Discipline of Market Leaders: Choose your Customers, Narrow your Focus, Dominate your Market* (Addison-Wesley 1995).

- Jim Collins describes the hedgehog concept in *Good to Great: Why Some Companies Make the Leap . . . and Others Don't* (Harper Collins, 2001).

- Jim Collins, *Turning the Flywheel: A Monograph to Accompany Good to Great* (Harper Business, 2019).

- "How New Mexico Is Beating the Virus" was published at https://www.nytimes.com/2020/05/01/opinion/new-mexico-coronavirus-curve.html.

- Allan Chochinov, "Change Everything You Hate About Meetings with This One Single Word" (https://productsofdesign.sva.edu/blog/nomeeting, 2018).

Part 5

- Paul Zak, "Why Your Brain Loves Good Storytelling" *Harvard Business Review* (2014) (https://hbr.org/2014/10/why-your-brain-loves-good-storytelling).

- Andrew Stanton's TED talk on storytelling can be found at https://www.ted.com/talks/andrew_stanton_the_clues_to_a_great_story.

- Roger Martin, "Help Leaders Be Less Useless at Strategy" (*Harvard Business Review,* May 2014).

Part 6

- John Boyd's OODA loop is described in "A Discourse on Winning and Losing" (*Maxwell Air Force Base, AL: Air University Library Document No. M-U 43947, 1987*).

- Carissa Carter, "Let's Stop Talking about THE Design Process," *Medium*, October 6, 2016 (https://medium.com/stanford-d-school/lets-stop-talking-about-the-design-process-7446e52c13e8).

- Blaise Pascal, *Lettres provincials* (1656-1657).

- Tom Peters writes that the one-page memo tradition goes back to Richard Deupree, past president of P&G, in *In Search of Excellence: Lessons from America's Best Run Companies* (Harper & Row, 1982).

- Osmo A. Wiio (1978). *Wiion lait ja vähän muidenkin* [Wiio's laws and some others]. Weilin+Göös.

- Lin-Manuel Miranda is the creator and original Broadway star of *Hamilton: An American Musical.*

The FrameShifting Lexicon

Frame */frām/ (noun):* A particular lens for defining an opportunity or looking at a problem or challenge.

Framing */frāmiNG/ (verb):* The activity of developing a frame; can be implicit or explicit depending on the individual.

Framework */frām wərk/ (noun):* A codified way to organize thinking and assess a problem; provides structure and promotes discipline. Specific methods and tools are often linked to the overarching framework.

FrameMaster */frām mastər/ (noun):* An archetype in organizations focused on one particular framework; has achieved mastery and helps others adopt the framework.

FrameSeeker */frām sēkər/ (noun):* An archetype who avidly reads, attends conferences and events, scanning external resources to find new frameworks and bring them into practice.

FrameBuilder */frām bildər/ (noun):* An archetype, typically external to an organization, who has considerable skill in a particular problem area and has designed a framework to address it.

FreeRadical */frē ra-di-kəl/ (noun):* An archetype within an organization who likes to jump right into problem solving; often a natural brainstormer who prefers unstructured thinking and finds frameworks constraining.

FrameShifting */frām SHiftiNG/ (verb):* A unique process for looking at problems or opportunities from multiple perspectives to develop a clear, unambiguous frame that can be matched to an appropriate framework; a breakthrough set of activities that transforms "swirl" into productive problem solving that yields innovative solutions. [—*FrameShift*, —*FrameShifted*]

Collaborate */kə- la-bə- rāt/ (verb):* To work jointly with others or together, especially in an intellectual endeavor. [From the Latin: col (together) + laborare (to work)]

FrameShifter */frām SHiftər/ (noun):* A leadership meta-archetype that embraces the philosophies and mindset of FrameShifting. Alert and aware, uses FrameShifting methods to discover powerful frames and collaborate with other archetypes to structure problem solving with the best-fit framework.

Acknowledgments

We are grateful to all those who have helped shape the ideas found on these pages—our clients, colleagues, and friends. Our writing partnership has benefitted tremendously from our own complementary skills and perspectives, and also from a small cadre of individuals who each contributed significantly to this endeavor. They are our posse.

Without Melissa Quinn, this book would never have come to be. She tells her story of meeting Alison for coffee in the Foreword. Alison remembers an earlier meeting at Deloitte, following an introduction by Melissa's husband, Brian. They met at the end of the day, and Alison was amazed by Melissa's openness, her insights about leading innovation, and her incredible generosity. It has been a privilege to remain in her circle and to benefit from her continual guidance, encouragement, and game-changing feedback.

Philip Kotler was indeed the first spark for this book. The author of more than fifty books, Dr. Kotler is widely regarded as "The Father of Marketing" and revered by all who were influenced by his work and teaching at the Kellogg School of Management at Northwestern University—Alison's alma mater. She was thrilled to meet him for the first time at the Kellogg Innovation Network conference in 2014. Alison still has the selfie that they took that memorable day.

We would also like to extend our heartfelt thank-you to our mutual clients and friends at Steelcase, without whom we would never have met. We have learned as much from you as we hope you have learned from us. In particular we want to acknowledge Bob Krestakos and Matt Mead for their trust and encouragement and for all the great stories we brought to life; Donna Flynn, who graciously offered to read and provide stellar feedback to the manuscript; and especially Sara Armbruster, for the initial introduction to Steelcase, and her unwavering confidence in the possibilities to solve tough problems together.

Thank you also to our manuscript editors and readers. Mary Anna Rodabaugh at RTC (www.roundtablecompanies.com) provided the first set of editor's eyes on an early version of the manuscript, and her input resulted in a restructuring of the narrative. Freelance editor Molly Bentsen generously provided "editorial proofreading" in the late stages of our book. A gem, she brings attention to detail to a whole new level. Valerie Valentine provided the last set of eyes on our manuscript and made important final edits. Finally, thank you to Laurel Romanella, for her legal work on our behalf as well as for her encouraging feedback on our manuscript.

We are also delighted with the work of Julie Karen Hodgins, our incredibly talented book designer who is responsible for the book cover and interior design of the pages. She writes frequently on book design and production at www.juliekaren.com.

Lastly, and most importantly, we are especially grateful to our loved ones. Thank you to Jim Heiser, for long walks in deep discussion and for coining the term FrameShifting. Thank you to Michael Heiser, for understanding the writing process as FrameShifting in practice and, together with Allison Nordstrom, for helping develop the archetype quiz. And thank you to Sidney Shaw, for his insight, encouragement, and unwavering support.

About the Authors

Alison Heiser is principal of Alison Heiser Associates, LLC, a strategy and innovation consultancy helping clients with "wicked problems" that require deep thinking and imagining new business models.

Alison has deep experience developing and leading implementation of forward-leaning strategies that deliver significant bottom-line results across a variety of industries and business situations. She is a talented change agent in organizations seeking to step change innovation and identify strategies for growth. Prior to consulting, she was a senior executive at several blue chip companies, engaging multiple consultants over the years. This gave her experience with a host of highly relevant frameworks to draw upon in her role reversal to consulting. Her corporate experience as a leader and consultant includes P&G, LensCrafters, Michelin, Accenture, Microsoft, BASF, Steelcase and many others.

She honed her consulting experience at Accenture, leading marketing and customer strategy client engagements for Fortune 100 companies undertaking enterprise-wide customer transformation initiatives. In 2009, Alison Heiser Associates launched with a small group of clients to bring marketing and strategy to CEOs leading mid-cap companies and privately held family-owned businesses. She was keenly focused on listening to clients talk about their issues, and often able to reframe these conversations into clearly defined challenges. Today, the business has expanded to serve leaders in nonprofit organizations and maintains strong relationships with her original clients.

Alison earned her MBA from the Kellogg School of Management at Northwestern University, and her BS in Communications from the University of Illinois at Urbana-Champaign. Alison lives on a tree farm in northern Wisconsin with her husband Jim and their ridiculously spoiled rescue pup Nala. Their son Michael is a technology consultant and lives in Chicago.

www.alisonheiserassociates.com

Mary O'Connor Shaw leads 360 Shaw Communications Inc., a consulting firm that helps business leaders craft powerful stories.

Mary speaks the language of business fluently. She is exceptionally adept at synthesizing complex—often highly technical—concepts into clever, hand-drawn illustrations that foster collaboration and inspire innovation.

Mary is also an experienced writer and trainer. She has developed many unique programs, including "Antibiotics & You," which earned the Centers for Disease Control and Prevention (CDC) Award for Excellence. Her latest workshop, "Learn to Draw with Mary Shaw," is a visual storytelling how-to course for business professionals.

Mary makes her home on a farm in West Michigan with her husband Sidney and their free-ranging flock of ridiculously spoiled laying hens.

www.360shaw.com

Thank you for reading FrameShifting

Please share your impressions
on social media using our hashtags and handles:

#FrameShifting
@FrameShifter
@AlisonAHA

For a downloadable FrameShifting Map
and additional resources, please visit:

www.frameshifting.org

*If you enjoyed this book, please consider writing
a review with your honest impressions on
Amazon, Goodreads, or the platform of your choosing.
Your feedback is incredibly valuable for helping
independent authors like us to reach a wider audience.*

Made in the USA
Coppell, TX
12 October 2023

22759580R00079